WHAT "JOY STUDY" PARTICIPANTS ARE SAYING . . .

"Jackie's exercises are so simple, you think they can't do a thing. I would compare them to trying to watch a flower open. Watch, and it doesn't seem to move. Then you blink your eyes, and it is in full bloom. In the same way, the exercises seem so very small. Then, one day you begin to see real changes in your life." —Madelyn B., Jefferson, Maryland

"I felt the biggest benefit of the joy exercises long after the study concluded. When my life descended into a whirlwind, I had a newfound sense that joy would return to me. I believe now and forever that joy permanently resides in me." —Celeste T., Durham, North Carolina

"During a period of difficult career changes, these exercises helped me stay positively focused and open to life's amazing possibilities. The tools were simple—focus on the joy that already existed in my life, and take daily responsibility for increasing my own joy. The results were profound!"
—Gene S., Danville, Pennsylvania

"Gratitude and appreciation for even the smallest of things can turn a negative outlook into one that is more positive, freeing you from emotions that are weighing you down. The 'joy' exercises taught me to look for the good in every moment!" —Deanna D., Lisbon, Ohio

"I use Appreciative Living principles and the exercises I learned in the study on a daily basis to shape my thinking and my focus, and to remind myself of my own power to envision and act toward the positive future I want. Beginning my day with the gratitude exercise (listing three things for which I am grateful) empowers me to face my day with a positive, appreciative attitude." —Wendy G., Raleigh, North Carolina

"At first, doing the exercises took some concentration and commitment. They soon became a wonderful part of my day, setting it up in a positive and grateful way that carried throughout the day. When I have an early appointment or am running late and do not do the exercises, my day seems to be offtrack and there are challenges I wish to avoid. I still do the exercises regularly, and can honestly say they have increased the joy in my life and continue to." —*Rita D., Ashland, Ohio*

"The reflection and inner peace of building on the power of joy each morning brought about a positive change and motivating energy to my daily living." —*Fred P., Columbus, Ohio*

The Joy of Appreciative Living

JEREMY P. TARCHER/PENGUIN

a member of Penguin Group (USA) Inc.

NEW YORK

THE JOY OF

{ Appreciative }

LIVING

Your 28-Day Plan to Greater Happiness
in 3 Incredibly Easy Steps

Jacqueline Kelm

JEREMY P. TARCHER/PENGUIN
Published by the Penguin Group
Penguin Group (USA) Inc., 375 Hudson Street, New York, New York 10014, USA •
Penguin Group (Canada), 90 Eglinton Avenue East, Suite 700, Toronto, Ontario
M4P 2Y3, Canada (a division of Pearson Canada Inc.) • Penguin Books Ltd,
80 Strand, London WC2R oRL, England • Penguin Ireland, 25 St Stephen's Green,
Dublin 2, Ireland (a division of Penguin Books Ltd) • Penguin Group (Australia),
250 Camberwell Road, Camberwell, Victoria 3124, Australia (a division of
Pearson Australia Group Pty Ltd) • Penguin Books India Pvt Ltd, 11 Community Centre,
Panchsheel Park, New Delhi—110 017, India • Penguin Group (NZ),
67 Apollo Drive, Rosedale, North Shore 0632, New Zealand (a division of
Pearson New Zealand Ltd) • Penguin Books (South Africa) (Pty) Ltd,
24 Sturdee Avenue, Rosebank, Johannesburg 2196, South Africa

Penguin Books Ltd, Registered Offices: 80 Strand, London WC2R oRL, England

Most Tarcher/Penguin books are available at special quantity discounts for bulk purchase
for sales promotions, premiums, fund-raising, and educational needs. Special books or
book excerpts also can be created to fit specific needs. For details, write Penguin Group
(USA) Inc. Special Markets, 375 Hudson Street, New York, NY 10014.

Library of Congress Cataloging-in-Publication Data
Kelm, Jacqueline Bascobert.
The joy of appreciative living: your 28-day plan to greater
happiness in 3 incredibly easy steps / Jacqueline Kelm.
p.   cm.
Includes bibliographical references and index.
ISBN 978-1-58542-660-7
1. Gratitude.   2. Joy.   3. Happiness.   4. Positive psychology.   I. Title.
BF575.G68K45   2009   2008040674
152.4'2—dc22

Printed in the United States of America
1   3   5   7   9   10   8   6   4   2

Book design by Jennifer Ann Daddio/Bookmark Design & Media Inc.

Neither the publisher nor the author is engaged in rendering professional advice or
services to the individual reader. The ideas, procedures, and suggestions contained in
this book are not intended as a substitute for consulting with a physician. All matters
regarding your health require medical supervision. Neither the author nor the publisher
shall be liable or responsible for any loss or damage allegedly arising from any information or suggestion in this book.

While the author has made every effort to provide accurate telephone numbers and
Internet addresses at the time of publication, neither the publisher nor the author
assumes any responsibility for errors, or for changes that occur after publication. Further, the publisher does not have any control over and does not assume any responsibility
for author or third-party websites or their content.

{ Contents }

Part Two: What You Need to Do

Appendices

An Inquiry into Joy

David Cooperrider

I love the word *joy,* and it immediately reminds me of a story, partly unsettling but enormously telling. A colleague in the positive psychology movement talks about it as "the Beethoven Factor":

> *There stood Beethoven, gravely ill and totally deaf. Eyes closed, he kept conducting the orchestra even after they had ceased their performance and the audience had risen to its feet in thunderous applause. As a singer stepped from the choir to turn him around to see those whose shouts of bravo resonated throughout the concert hall, tears of elation filled his eyes. Perhaps the worst loss a composer could experience had been the catalyst for a remarkable adaptive creativity that allowed him to transcend his tortures to become immersed in the thrill of*

*conducting the premiere of his Ninth Symphony, the "Ode
to Joy."* [1]

At that moment, and not only in spite of but because of the way
he related to his adversity, Beethoven experienced a moment to
rejoice that inspires us all. Why? Because this story reminds us
that human flourishing is not determined by external circumstances—even "bad" situations can be related to in ways that
make us happier, more alive, and more content than we ever
imagined possible. We participate, as makers of meaning, in the
creation and magnification of joy: We are all sculptors, authors,
and composers. Our lives, quite simply, are our most precious
projects. And a life of joy—if we want it—is ours to cultivate and
to cherish, to express and spread, and to discover and design.
This is the message of *The Joy of Appreciative Living.*

In this astonishing volume, Jackie Kelm shares the words
of wisdom of ordinary people who participated in an extraordinary research project dedicated to finding the equivalent
of a "pill for joy." Only there were no pills. Only questions and
inquiries, powerful positive questions, which, "taken" in easy
doses each day, created journeys of joy with progressive upward
spirals. The continuing expansion of joy in people's lives—even
breaking the ceiling of so-called happiness set points—went
on for months and is still continuing, way beyond the first
twenty-eight-day intervention. "I was shocked when the final
six-month results came in," writes Jackie. "The numerical data
from the study was incredible. . . . I knew I had found it: the
closest thing yet to a joy pill."

I know Jackie Kelm—she is an amazing student of life—and I
am sure her eyes were sparkling when she wrote those words. I

was privileged to teach and work with Jackie years ago when she was an MBA student studying economics, finance, and business strategy. She was the most curious and serious MBA student I ever encountered in all my years of teaching at the Weatherhead School of Management at Case Western Reserve University. I say all this because Jackie has combined all the analytic talent of an economist and all the pragmatic talent of a business manager to approach the seemingly unapproachable topic of joy in a way that makes it accessible, real, and absolutely pragmatic—no empty promises or ethereal mirages here!

The subtitle of this book, "Your 28-Day Plan to Greater Happiness in 3 Incredibly Easy Steps," is a bold assertion, especially "in 3 Incredibly Easy Steps." But it is true. Change, even dramatic change and transformation, is easier than we ever thought before—when it is approached in a positive, life-centric, appreciative way.

What Jackie Kelm does in this volume is to give us a method, a powerful set of tools, to make this kind of change an easy and accessible part of our lives. She does it by extending perhaps the most important principle of Appreciative Inquiry (AI), which says that human systems move in the direction of what they most persistently, authentically, and systematically ask questions about. In short, inquiry into joy—asking when is it most alive in us . . . or asking what's the smallest thing we can do today to increase the joy we want . . . or asking what does it look like in the future ideal joy-filled life—is the discovery spirit that will fill our lives with more joy, more possibility, than we ever thought possible. Appreciate joy, for what we appreciate appreciates.

This was Beethoven's secret. Composing a piece of music

is a lot like inquiry. The topic he chose? It was "Ode to Joy." Beethoven became what he focused on and studied, and so do we. His tears of elation were not because of the thunderous applause; in fact he could not hear it at all.

He thrived because he made a choice.

Read this book with care. It's more powerful than a pill. Take notice of moments of joy, especially the small ones. Study how joy suspends gravity. See if it has anything to do with beaming, shining, and glowing. Treasure the daily questions Jackie lifts up. Wonder about their possibilities. Delight in the joy of others. And continuously ask yourself: What happens to my relationships, indeed to the whole world around me, when I act, speak, and inquire from a place of joy?

Professor David Cooperrider
Case Western Reserve University
2008

{ Introduction }

*When I chose to laugh for no reason or look for the beauty
in everyday experiences, I felt my spirit rise. I felt released
from an anchor, allowing the day to bring joy rather than
chasing after it. It is like chasing butterflies. When you
run after them they are elusive. When you sit
still amid flowers they alight upon you.*
—Study participant

Let me be brief: All my life I wanted joy and I wanted it right away. If there had been a pill for joy, I would have taken it. I had been desperately seeking happiness my entire existence and had left a stream of self-help books, workshops, twelve-step programs, psychotherapists, and healers in my wake. And the draft was deep.

In the 1990s I was introduced to something called Appreciative Inquiry (AI), which was first conceptualized in the 1980s by business professor David Cooperrider while he was pursuing his doctorate at Case Western under the guidance of his Ph.D. adviser, Suresh Srivastva. Appreciative Inquiry is essentially a positive, strength-based approach to organizational change distinguished by "the co-evolutionary search for the best in people, their organizations, and the relevant world around them."[2] (For an overview of AI, see Appendix A: What Is Appreciative Inquiry?) Interest in this approach has been growing steadily, with use in organizations such as McDonald's, Wal-Mart, Roadway Express, Hunter Douglas, the United Nations, and a host of others.

I worked with Appreciative Inquiry as a management consultant for several years and was mesmerized by the power and effectiveness of this approach. I watched as departments and entire organizations transformed before my very eyes, and I began to wonder what would happen if it were applied to daily life.

In 2000 I began to do just that. I went deep into the principles of Appreciative Inquiry and translated these organizational change concepts into personal living. I also researched and integrated other positive approaches such as positive psychology, the law of attraction, and the new sciences. My life began to transform beyond anything I ever dreamed possible, and I called this philosophy Appreciative Living.

Appreciative Living changed my life. It affected every major area, from my career and marriage to my finances and parenting. In 2005 I wrote *Appreciative Living: The Principles of Appreciative Inquiry in Personal Life* to explain the philosophical and practical framework for this approach, and I continued to get happier and more joyful while helping others do the same. I loved my life and work, but it still seemed a bit complicated. There were multiple concepts and practices and a whole variety of ways to use them. Sometimes it was difficult to know where to start.

And then in the spring of 2006 I had a real epiphany. In the pages ahead I'll share the whole story, but I essentially uncovered a simple way to integrate *all* these positive-focused ideas into just three brief exercises to create meaningful, lasting joy. I then did a study with thirty people from across the United States to see how well the exercises worked, and the results simply blew me away. I asked participants to do the exercises for just twenty-eight days, and after that point twenty-nine out of the thirty participants rated themselves as being in the top "happy" half of the scale. The part that was even more astounding was that the group was still significantly happier six months later, even though most had stopped doing the exercises by that time! To top it off, the exercises took less than five minutes a day, plus fifteen minutes on the weekend. They were so simple I was able to do them with my six- and eight-year-old children, and they were flexible enough to fit into our busy schedules.

There are many paths to joy, but this book contains one of the fastest, simplest, and most effective ways to begin the journey. I'm reminded of a quote by Oliver Wendell Holmes: "I wouldn't give a fig for the simplicity on this side of complexity, but I would give my life for the simplicity on the other side of complexity." The exercises look deceivingly simple, but sit on the other side of complexity. You may have seen versions of some of them before, but the unique combination generates a synergy that greatly accelerates personal change. I'll explain more about how they are designed and how to do the exercises later in the book, but for now let me share a brief overview of what they are:

1. List three things you appreciate each day, and take a moment to feel your gratitude.
2. Each day answer this question: "What one thing can I do today, no matter how small, to increase my joy?"

3. Once a week do a fifteen-minute visioning exercise of
   your ideal, joy-filled life.

As simple as these exercises may look, you can expect to become
noticeably happier after practicing them for just twenty-eight
days. The exercises will open your eyes to how your thinking affects your experience. As you become aware of how your
thoughts move you further toward or away from joy, you will discover practical ways of creating happiness right now. If you go
beyond twenty-eight days and incorporate the exercises into your
daily routine, your possibilities for happiness will increase as
the awareness between your thinking and experience expands.

How to Use This Book

There are two primary ways to use this book. The first is to read
through it in its entirety and then do the exercises, which is what
I recommend. The first section provides a wealth of knowledge
and great stories about how joy works, and this information will
accelerate your progress tremendously. The second half of the
book gets into the details of what to do and how, and is equally
important in getting the most out of the exercises and keeping
up with them. And make sure you read the last two chapters,
which show you how to take these practices into your daily life
and create greater joy than you ever dreamed possible.

The second way to use this book is to begin doing the exercises as summarized in Appendix B: Exercise Summary, and
then go back and read the book while you are doing them. If you
are the kind of person who tends to act first and figure it out

later, this approach might work better for you. Either way you choose, you can receive more information about the program at www.AppreciativeLiving.com.

One final note as you begin reading. Throughout the book I interchange the words *happiness* and *joy*. In chapter 7 I explain their differences, but for simple ease of reading I will be using them both in the pages that follow.

In the end, you get to decide what joy is about for you. For some it's learning how to appreciate and experience the sheer bliss of living, and for others it's connecting to a deeper, more spiritual center. Joy is yours to discover, and practicing these simple steps will open the door for you.

Now on to the story of how people from across the United States became more joyful in twenty-eight days, and how you can do the same. It's a story with a very happy ending—yours.

Part One

WHAT YOU NEED TO
{ Know }

The Story Behind the Study

Doing the exercises is like internal feng shui.
—Study participant

It all began one ordinary summer afternoon while I was preparing an evening speech for a local spiritual community. I decided to speak about joy and was doing some research to build compelling ideas and gather juicy tidbits. I could not imagine I was about to stumble across an idea so profound it would change the entire course of my work.

All my work and writing until that point had been about helping people use Appreciative Living to create anything they wanted in their lives—whether it was greater peace, better relationships, or financial abundance. The principles I taught worked just as well for manifesting spiritual growth as they did for abundance, and I had developed tools and models to help people along.

So there I was, randomly picking up another book in

preparation for my speech. From the top of the pile I grabbed *Happiness Is a Choice* by Barry Neil Kaufman, which I had read a while back. I flipped through it again, looking for powerful examples to share, or perhaps an inspiring quote.

And then the strangest thing happened. As I scanned the book, I started to feel as if my brain were being rewired. Barry Kaufman's main point, which he continuously reiterates, is that *in order to be happy, you must make it the priority in your life*. It sounded so simple on the surface, but the more I thought about it, the more profound it became. And then I had an epiphany.

All of sudden, a whole new possibility burst forth. What if I could help people create joy just for the sake of creating joy? All my work up until this point treated joy as a by-product. In other words, I would help people build the career of their dreams, with the implied understanding that it would lead to more joy. Or I would help them improve their health with the idea that it would lead to greater happiness. It was always the assumed result of whatever change people wanted to make for the better. But what if I made joy the main event? What if I had people stop looking for the outer things that would create more joy, and simply had them *put joy first*?

Wow.

It was a fascinating concept, and I wrestled a bit with what it really meant. How exactly would you *put joy first*? I tried to figure out how to explain the idea to the audience, but more important, I wanted to figure out how it could be applied practically in daily living. I wanted to know how it actually could be done.

I sat back and considered everything I knew about personal change from all my work and research. I had never consid-

ered trying to help people create joy all by itself, but the more
I worked with it, the more profound and glaringly obvious it
became. I began designing an intervention focused exclusively
on joy, in the way I would design one focused on creating an ideal
life. I worked with a model I had created and used successfully
for long-term change.

A summary of the model is included in Appendix C: Appreciative Living 3-Step Model. It consists of three basic steps:
1. Appreciating What Is. 2. Imagining the Ideal. 3. Acting in
Alignment. I selected the one most effective and powerful exercise for the time invested from each step and tailored it to creating joy. Everyone is busy these days, and I knew that no one
would do the exercises if they weren't brief. At the same time
they needed to be effective, since I wanted them to have a lasting impact and not be just a surface experience.

I looked at the combination of exercises, almost in disbe-
lief. Why hadn't I thought to put them together like this before?
Now that I had done so, the synergy between them was so obvious. Chills began running throughout my body and I knew I
was onto something big. I could just feel the power of what was
before me and how it simplified and aligned everything I had
come to know so far. If this were a movie, it would be the time
where sunlight would burst through the windows and trumpets would sound. I couldn't wait to have my audience try out the
exercises. It was this last thought that caused the trumpets to
go flat.

It is a well-known fact that most people in an audience will
not do the exercises you suggest once they leave an event. Even if
a few did do the exercises, I would have no way to follow up and
find out how they worked. If this were a movie, it would be the

part where the music gets somber, and you begin to wonder how it will all work out.

So I sat there at my desk, wondering what to do. I only had four hours until I had to speak, and I was bound and determined to get the audience to *do* these exercises. At this point a quiet little voice spoke from deep inside, and it said something like this: "Why don't you do a study on how these exercises work and get people to sign up tonight?" Sometimes I don't want to listen to that little voice, and my first thought was, "That idea is insane."

At that point my inner voice turned into an inner dialogue. I thought to myself, "The last study I did was for my engineering thesis on heat transfer and air-flow properties of automotive heating and air-conditioning systems. How can I translate that study to one on joy? Even if I could figure it out, I only have four hours until I present. This is crazy." And then the voice from down deep spoke again and said, "Just do it. Tonight would be the perfect time to start." I continued to argue with myself and thought, "This is absurd. I don't even know what to measure. Airflow I can do, but how in the world do you measure joy?"

Now some of you may be wondering about this inner voice— it's a voice I experience as a deeper wisdom that lies within. It is a voice I am starting to hear more clearly, and even more recently, listening to. It was feeling particularly strong that day, so I decided to strike a deal.

I said to myself, "I only have four hours until I have to speak. If this is something I really must do, then point me to a joy measurement tool in the next ten minutes." So I went directly to my altar of worship: my bookshelf. Part of me was hoping to find what I asked for, while another was overwhelmed by what that would mean.

I pressed on with my mission and did a quick scan of the books with a strong research base. I was drawn to one called *Authentic Happiness* by University of Pennsylvania professor Martin Seligman, who is considered the father of positive psychology. I pulled the book from the shelf and it literally fell open to page fifteen, and guess what was there? It was a simple assessment tool psychologists and clinicians have used for measuring happiness. My mouth dropped open and my inner voice screamed, "I won! I won!" I began to sweat bullets.

In addition to getting everything ready for that evening, my husband, Jon, was out of town and I had to get my two children from elementary school and feed and love them. The next four hours were a blur as I pulled the study together, put dinner on the table, and wrote and printed handouts, assessments, and sign-up sheets. I had no idea what I was getting into, which was probably a good thing. The trumpets began to sound again.

That night I officially birthed my new focus on joy, and it was a resounding success. At the end of the presentation I sent around a clipboard for people to sign up for what I ended up calling the "It's All About Joy" Study. It would begin a few weeks later and run for twenty-eight days, requiring participants to do the three brief exercises I described in the presentation. Nine people volunteered on the spot.

I then decided to announce the study to my small e-mail list, and within two days I had forty-five participants, with twenty on the waiting list. I had trouble closing the study down and continued to receive e-mails for months afterward from people wanting to participate. The response was overwhelming, and I knew I was onto something. I had people from all over the United States, including Alaska, and one from Canada.

I couldn't wait to get started. I knew these exercises were going to change people's lives, but I was completely unprepared for what was to follow.

Fast-forward three months. It was Saturday night and Jon and I were waiting for a table in a crowded restaurant lounge. I was thinking about the study; the numbers for the first half were in, and they looked amazing. The unhappiest people tended to have the biggest change, which I guess makes sense when you think about it. They had a lot more room for improvement than people who were already fairly happy to begin with. (For a detailed write-up of the results see Appendix H: Joy Study Results Summary.)

I did some simple calculations on the data to determine average changes, but my statistics skills are fuzzier than I'd like to admit. I was hoping to complete an initial write-up in the next few weeks, but was struggling through the statistical calculations to determine whether the results were mathematically significant. And then the universe intervened.

I happened to strike up a conversation with a woman sitting next to me in the restaurant lounge, who just happened to be a statistics professor at North Carolina State University. So I started blurting out my study results and asking her which statistical tests I should run. After a good half hour of napkin scratching, with lots of blank stares from me, she finally ended up doing the analysis in her office and sending me the results. Her name is Tamara Young, and she was a life saver.

The study results came back as being significant, so I could statistically claim that the exercises worked. People did get happier as a result of doing them, and I had the data to back it up.

Fast-forward several more months. I e-mailed Tamara to tell her the final results would be in shortly, but that I probably would not need her to do any calculations. After all, it had been six months since the study began and I couldn't imagine people were still experiencing the effects of the initial exercises. On top of that, the study had started in the "happy" month of July, and this final data point was being taken in the "unhappy" month of January.

While it may seem intuitively obvious that we are happier in some months than others, University of Cardiff psychologist Dr. Cliff Arnall actually has a formula for calculating the most depressing and happiest days in the United Kingdom.[3] The actual dates vary by a day or two each year, and are determined by factors such as weather, debt, social interaction, and day of the week. During the time of the study, the most depressing day was calculated to be January 22, which is about the time we get that whopping credit card statement and break our New Year's resolutions all in one fell swoop. The happiest day that year was June 23.[4] I took the final data point on January 14, so if you think there is anything to Dr. Arnall's calculations, I was only about a week off of picking the worst possible time to end the study.

That is part of the reason I was so shocked when the final six month results came in. Not only was there a marked improvement in people's happiness since the study began, but every person was still in the happy part of the scale, except for one. The overall average happiness of the group was at an all-time high! My one regret in the whole experience is that I stopped taking data after six months.

Frankly, I couldn't believe the results, so I e-mailed all the people who started off as "unhappy" in the study to ask them about their experience. I wrote that their results were incredible, and I needed to know if there was anything else going on to explain it. My reputation was at stake, and I wanted to be sure their increase in joy was really a result of doing the exercises and not something else...like winning the lottery. Here are a few examples of what they wrote:

> *In my mind, there is no doubt that the exercises were the seeds that germinated into the harvest of well-being I feel today. When I started actively looking for those little things for which to feel grateful I found even greater things, and with that came clearer thinking.*

> *I attribute my change in attitude with spending the time thinking positive thoughts and feeling positive feelings brought on by the exercises. . . . For me, even when I got distressed, the simple memory of how good I could feel (when I focused on the positive) was enough to allow me to believe that the bad times would truly meet a "this too shall pass" moment.*

> *I think the joy study was part of a turning point for me in trying to have a positive outlook and allowing myself to enjoy life more. I'm still a long way from where I want to be, but the skills I learned from you have definitely helped and given me some good perspective. Thank you.*

> *I believe that my increase was based on the exercises.*

All of the people responded to me, essentially saying the same thing—the exercises either had directly contributed to feeling more joyful while they were doing them, or had prompted them to take action in some way that made their lives better. The fact that twenty out of the thirty participants continued doing some form of the exercises on their own after the twenty-eight days suggests that most people found them powerful. After six months almost half the group was still doing some of them occasionally. There was only one person in the study who said the exercises did not seem to make much difference, so I decided that the experience of twenty-nine out of thirty people was a pretty safe foundation on which to stake a claim.

At this point I felt confident that these exercises really worked, and I started sharing them with others. Workshop participants tried them, as did neighbors, friends, and people browsing my website. More and more stories poured in of people's lives changing for the better, and I haven't even told you the best part of all.

The numerical data from the study was incredible, showing that people got significantly happier by doing the exercises. While that information was inspiring, it didn't hold a candle to the qualitative data. I interviewed most of the participants by phone after the study was over and received phone calls and e-mails from eager people outside the study who had tried some of the exercises on their own. I was bowled over by the incredible depth and power of the experiences people shared.

Most amazing was the fact that their insights were consistent with the Five Principles of Appreciative Inquiry. Many people in the study knew nothing of these principles, and yet they were discovering the key ideas on their own and living them.

I summarized their learnings about joy and mapped them onto the original Appreciative Inquiry principles as follows:

1. The Constructionist Principle: Change Your Stories to Change Your Life
2. The Poetic Principle: Look for Joy in All the Right Places
3. The Simultaneity Principle: Harness the Power of Questions
4. The Anticipatory Principle: Act from Inspiration Rather Than Desperation
5. The Positive Principle: Be Upward Trendy

In the chapters ahead I'll go into an in-depth description of these Five Principles and you will see what participants discovered about joy within this framework. These insights will accelerate the progress of your own joy journey, and you will have a much better understanding of how the exercises work when you get to them in chapter 8.

It was exhilarating to watch the lightbulb come on as people began to see how joy really worked in their lives, and to watch the light glow brighter as they got better at creating it. The fact that participants were able to significantly shift their happiness level and instinctively understand the appreciative principles from the exercises went way beyond my expectations for what was possible. That was it. I had found it: the closest thing yet to a joy pill.

{ 2 }

I. The Constructionist Principle: Change Your Stories to Change Your Life

The possibilities for framing a day are endless. If we don't make
a conscious effort to decide, if we leave it up to the winds, it's like
seaweed in the ocean. It goes wherever the current takes it. We
need to make conscious choices and deliberately frame our day.
—Study participant

I have to confess. These next five chapters are my favorites as they contain the stories, insights, and wisdom people gleaned from doing the joy exercises. The chapters are neatly packaged into the five original principles of Appreciative Inquiry, resulting in a unique and refreshing way to look at joy. This information will greatly accelerate your own journey as you pick up where these thirty people left off.

In the early 1990s David Cooperrider created the five principles of the Appreciative Inquiry philosophy.[5] Five additional principles have been suggested over the years by AI practioners, but I'll only talk about the original five here. I go into depth on all ten principles in my first book, *Appreciative Living.*[6]

The first principle is the Constructionist Principle; its

essential idea is that we continuously create or construct stories about what is happening in our lives. The reality we experience is completely subjective, and it is seen through the unique lenses and filters through which we view the world. This principle underlies all the others and is at the heart of understanding Appreciative Inquiry.

I had been looking for a great example to illustrate how this principle works, and the study provided a most amazing one. Here is what happened.

There were two people in the study who simultaneously witnessed a traumatic event, and the stories they told were strongly contrasting. Here is what the first person wrote:

> I witnessed a man in a horrible industrial accident at my workplace. I stood there as he begged for relief and screamed in pain as people tried to help and waited for the ambulance. I couldn't move. I didn't do anything. For about a week after that I was barely functional. I ate, did my work, and slept. I couldn't do my joy journal at that time. Joy seemed so very far away and not something that I deserved.

In this story, we see a woman describe the pain and anguish of witnessing a traumatic event. What she chooses to notice and the meaning she makes of it all is a product of her past experiences and beliefs and the thinking patterns she has developed over time. Now consider the story told by the second person:

> I witnessed a serious accident in which a coworker friend of mine was badly injured in an industrial accident. It happened in a large group and was very traumatic for everyone involved.

However, what was really remarkable was that the incident was a catalyst for a lot of really incredibly wonderful things. First, the people involved did a phenomenal job of taking care of him and each other to deal with the situation both immediately and in the weeks that followed (this happened at the end of the first week of the study). Second, in caring for my friend during his recovery, I found myself put on the path to an entirely new chapter of my life, as the experience has prompted me to go to nursing school. . . . And strange as it may sound, there were many moments of pure joy throughout that whole ordeal, even for my friend, who has already recovered far beyond his doctor's expectations!

Consider these two accounts of the same event. In the first scenario the person could barely function the following week, while the second experienced moments of pure joy. Both were in the same situation, but they had completely different experiences and perspectives about what happened. This is a classic illustration of the constructionist principle: *We live in the world our stories create.*

We continuously make up stories about what is going on and what it all means, and no two of us create the same stories. We filter situations and people and everything that happens through the lenses of the unique assumptions and beliefs we've adopted from our families, culture, school, media, neighbors, friends, jobs, gas station attendants, telemarketers, and every other person, plant, animal, rock, and institution with which we have had contact. If I once had a horrible experience with a stray dog, the memory of that event will color my story the next time I come in contact with a stray dog. I will feel fear as I project my negative past stories onto my current experience. Conversely, if my previous experience with stray dogs is loving, the sight of a stray dog will elicit an entirely different story and felt response.

Each of us views the world through a set of glasses or filters that are as unique as snowflakes. If you go back to the stories of the industrial accident, you see how different they can be. The important point is that the stories we make up about our lives are just that: stories. They are just one perspective of what is happening.

The story of the first woman who was paralyzed with fear may be closer to what the majority might think, in the sense that most of us would have categorized this as a "bad" experience. In our culture we primarily learn to pay attention to what is wrong, and we spend a lot of time in the negative emotions surrounding a situation.

The experience of the second woman is remarkable; I bet most of us would have been hard-pressed to find joy in the midst of what happened. It is quite radical to see joy while others are in pain; this woman has an exceptional way of viewing the world. You can tell she is aware of her unique perception by the way she uses the words "strange as it may sound" to describe her joy. People often ask me what Appreciative Living is; I'd like to suggest that this woman embodies Appreciative Living, and that her story demonstrates it beautifully. Appreciative Living is a paradigm or set of filters in which you naturally tend to see the positive aspects and potential in what is happening, and out of it you create something even better. It is learning to find what's right and to turn lemons into lemonade.

Notice that Appreciative Living is not about ignoring the bad. The second woman did not disregard what was going on or somehow try to minimize the seriousness of what she saw. She was fully aware of the gravity of the situation and was right there helping.

And consider how effectively she responded. Ignoring the bad
in a situation or "wearing rose-colored glasses" is called denial.
Appreciative Living is not about ignoring the bad, but accepting
it while deliberately looking for the inherent strengths, gifts,
and positive possibilities in the situation. It is seeing all of what's
there, within an appreciative framework. As Noelle Nelson and
Jeannine Calaba state in their book *The Power of Appreciation*, it
is "seeing the best in others without being blind to their weak-
nesses, [and] . . . perceiving the greatest possible good in all situations while being alert to what will and won't work for you."[7]

It is knowing there is more than one story about what is
going on, and looking for the greater possibilities that are also
present. Can you see how neither one of these accident stories
was "right" in the absolute sense? Each perspective was the true
felt experience for each person. If you had been there, you would
have perceived it differently. The point is to recognize that
we are *creating* our life experience with our thinking; it is not
something that is *happening* to us. This was an essential realization for several joy study participants:

> *The biggest insight I had was that I have the ability to create
> my own happiness every morning and share it with others.*

> *The biggest learning I had was moving from a life of default
> to saying I can design my life, deconstructing what I had con-
> structed (divorce, job elimination, etc.). It's like building a
> house—first you have to dig a big hole.*

People began to see that they were responsible for creating
their happiness, and it was done through their thinking. They

realized joy was not dependent on other people or the situations in which they found themselves, but in how they decided to think about those situations. One woman in particular had a profound insight, as she realized that her experience with her husband had little to do with him and everything to do with herself:

> *The one thing I came away with was my husband doesn't make me happy. He just does what he's going to do. Intellectually I get that, but I haven't gotten that on an emotional level. Now I get that he's going to do what he's going to do, and I'm responsible for how I respond to him. If I let him impact me, it's not his fault.*

I consider this a very advanced insight, and most of us would be lucky to grasp the idea, let alone experience it. The last sentence is particularly profound: *If I let him impact me, it's not his fault.* Not only does this woman see that she is solely responsible for framing her interactions, but on the off chance she lets in a little turmoil, she accepts it as a lapse in her process and not a fault of his.

When I showed this last quote to a friend of mine, he was mortified. He said, "That's awful. I would never want to get to the point where other people do not 'impact' me, because then I would not feel the good things either." Let me stop for a moment here and clarify a very important point: Staying joyful in difficult situations and not letting others bother us is not about disconnecting from people or ignoring them in any way. It is about realizing that it is *our story* that is disconnecting us from the other person, and we are responsible for our story.

It is realizing that the negative emotions we are experiencing are coming from our own thoughts, not other people. Our negative story is pushing us away from the other person and we need to find something to value or love or appreciate if we want to get closer. We can step back, look at the story that is running, and intentionally shift it in ways that serve us better. Again, this does not mean we separate from other people, just our stories. In fact, the more we are able to detach from our negative stories and see them as "just stories," the easier it is to create the space for more positive stories to emerge. It is the anger, fear, and mistrust in our negative stories that keep us from connecting; these are the greatest obstacles we have in building close relationships.

Learning to separate from our stories and look in on them is an essential skill for creating happiness.[8] Joyful relationships are molded in our thinking, and we alone are the artists of our craft. That reminds me of a variation of the serenity prayer a friend of mine shared:

> *Grant me the serenity to accept the people I cannot change,*
> *the courage to change the one I can,*
> *and the wisdom to know it's me.*

One of the keys to finding joy is owning the responsibility within rather than trying to find it without. It is another one of those concepts that is easier said than done. At times I still find myself wanting to blame others instead of going inside my story and looking at my part. We have a lot of years of putting responsibility outside ourselves, and these thinking habits take time to undo. With repeated practice we can create new patterns to help us turn the mirror around more quickly, so we can look to our stories for answers. This is where we find our joy.

A friend of mine loves dogs, and he uses dog analogies with difficult people to help shift his negative stories. When he meets a person he finds distasteful, he selects a particular breed of dog he believes symbolizes that person's personality. He then imagines the person as this type of dog, and it changes the relationship entirely. Before you write this off as some perverse mind game, let's look closer.

There was a woman who really bothered him whom he described as a whiny, hyper, obnoxious, non-stop talker who was incredibly self-centered. She spoke incessantly about herself, her children, her issues, her, her, her. He had a hard time being in her presence and found her utterly distasteful. All this changed once he did his dog trick.

One day he decided to imagine her as a tiny little Chihuahua dancing around with a jangly collar, jingling and yipping and acting uppity. Once he saw her in this role, he realized she was just doing what Chihuahuas do. He would watch her prance and flit around, which allowed him to accept this as simple Chihuahua behavior. As he viewed her in this light, he actually started to enjoy her company and began to see her good traits. He came to see she had a good heart, loved her family deeply, and was a delightful woman underneath all her antics. By changing his negative story of her to something more positive, he started to like her and connect with her.

A key point is that he found a way to accept her behavior and stopped expecting her to be anything other than what she was. You might find his associating the woman with a dog a bit crass, but is it really any worse than viewing her as obnoxious, whiny, and self-centered? His dog images act like bridges to allow him to move his stories in a positive direction. It is a tool he uses in difficult relationships, and as the relationships improve, he can let go of the dog images and move into stories that focus on the newfound positive traits he had been blind to earlier.

So much of our anger and frustration with others comes from wanting and expecting them to be something other than what they are. We want to rewrite their identities and make them into the image and likeness of what we think is best. Once we find a way to love and accept them where they are, we really connect and make way for a whole new relationship to open up. There's a side benefit to this as well. Learning to love and accept others is a sneaky way to do it for ourselves.

As some of the study participants realized they were responsible for creating their happiness with their thinking, an interesting realization emerged: They were not responsible for the happiness of others. It became clear that each of us has to create our own joy, and no one else can do it for us. Two people commented specifically on this:

> One of the key learnings I had was to be responsible for myself. I used to feel responsible for the happiness of my husband, my mother, the kids—I was trying to make everyone happy. They have to find their own thing. I am not responsible for anyone else besides myself. It makes me very happy. I feel so free.

> When I started writing down the one thing I could do to increase my joy I found I was still very much attempting to control not only my life, but the lives of those around me.

The point is not to turn narcissistic and forget about everyone else, but to realize where we have control and where we don't.

The happiness of other people is fundamentally outside our control. We can influence and exert force to "make" other people physically do certain things, but we cannot get into their heads and rearrange their thinking. Joy is created from the inside, and the insides of others are off limits to us.

It actually can be quite liberating to let go of trying to make other people happy. Again, to clarify, it does not mean we ignore others or stop caring about them. It means we love and support them as much as humanly possible, but we stop taking responsibility for their experience. We let them live their lives and encourage them as best we can to find their own joy journey so we can get on with the business of finding ours. In the words of Mahatma Gandhi, "Be the change you wish to see in the world."

In the end, it all comes back to us. As you do the exercises you'll come to realize that you alone create your happiness with your thoughts, and no one else can do it for you. As you learn to look for the good so you can shift your stories and reframe them in an appreciative way, a whole new wonderful story opens up right alongside the one you're currently living.

The Constructionist Principle suggests that reality is subjective, and we live in the world we create with our stories. A happier life comes from happier stories, and the next four principles tell us how it's done.

One of my favorite quotes is by James Branch Cabell: "The optimist proclaims we live in the best of all possible worlds, and the pessimist fears this is true." This quote epitomizes Appreciative Living, but it also begs the question "What world do you live in?" A more inspiring question is "What world do you want to live in?" That, my friends, is what the rest of this book is all about.

3

II. The Poetic Principle: Look for Joy in All the Right Places

*Joy is the art of finding pleasure in the simple moments
of life, whether they are large or small. It is in the
looking for joy that one finds it.*
—*Study participant*

The second principle in Appreciative Inquiry is the Poetic Principle. It suggests that we can find whatever we want in any situation, and whatever we choose to notice is fateful. All is present in every moment, from love to fear, good to bad, beautiful to ugly, joy to sorrow. Whatever we focus on from the unbounded possibilities defines our experience. In this sense reality is like poetry; it can be written in any manner conceivable and is open to infinite interpretations.

The Poetic Principle stems from the Constructionist Principle, as does each of the remaining principles. The Constructionist Principle broadly states that reality is created through our stories about what is happening, and in that sense it is completely subjective. The Poetic Principle takes it a step further, suggesting that each moment is replete with an infinite array of possibilities and what we choose to notice becomes our experience. Whatever we focus on will grow.

Going back to the previous chapter and the story of the two women who witnessed an industrial accident, you'll recall they each found very different things in the same situation. One woman wrote how the man "begged for help and screamed in pain," and her resulting experience included a lot of fear and pain. The other woman wrote about the traumatic event, but also commented on how "the people involved did a phenomenal job of taking care of him and each other to deal with the situation." Her focus on cooperation and support made for an experience that included moments of pure joy.

We have a choice about where to place our attention in any situation, and our choice is fateful. Whatever we focus on becomes a bigger part of our experience. You can liken it to adjusting the lens on a camera as you move from the background to close up, bringing certain things into focus while others go out. Where we choose to focus our lens is a culturally developed, patterned response we have created over time, and it sits on top of the beliefs and assumptions we have adopted from the myriad influences around us. Our families, friends, communities, culture, and institutions all have a say in what is important for us to pay attention to, and we generally adopt their suggestions. It is largely an unconscious process unless we intentionally pull it into our awareness.

Although everything is present in every moment, as German economist E. F. Schumacher says, "We can only see what we have grown an eye to see." In other words, we are conditioned to view reality in a certain way, and it is difficult and, in some cases, impossible for us to see it any other way. It takes effort to venture off the path into unknown territory, but that is what is required if we want to see something new.

I saw this clearly one day with my daughter when she was seven. She wanted to write her own book, and asked if I would type it into the computer for her as she told me what she wanted to say. I agreed, and it became a special activity the two of us would do together here and there over the course of a year or so. The title of her book was *How to Make Friends,* and chapters included "Exploding with Friends," "How to Stand Up," "How to Deal with Scary Thoughts," and "What to Do if You Live in a Place with No Kids." She would share her wisdom for each chapter out loud, and I took a vow of silence to type exactly what she said without comment. I would type away for several paragraphs each sitting, and over time we ended up with about four single-spaced pages for each chapter. That is, until we got to chapter 7.

Something unusual happened in chapter 7. I typed one paragraph, and then my daughter fell silent. I broke my vow to stay out of it all and started asking questions to try to help her through her "writer's block," but she simply could not come up with anything else to add. While she had more than four single-spaced pages for all of the other chapters, she had not "grown an eye to see" beyond a single paragraph for this topic. I told her we could work together to find more material, but she was not interested. So we simply moved on to the next chapter. It was a brilliant illustration of how we literally can only see what we have learned to see, and cannot see beyond it *unless we choose to.* Oh, by the way, the title of the one-paragraph chapter was "Learning to Like Your Brother or Sister." In case you are curious, I'm reprinting it here with her permission:

If you think your little brother or sister is really, really annoying like me, you might as well start off each day with either thinking something up that's good about your brother or sister, or else writing five things you like about them. Another thing you can do is try letting them do whatever they want, and then they might become nicer and do what you want.

I'm happy to report that several months later she did *choose* to go back and finish the chapter, but the general idea is that we all have our blind spots. Going back again to the industrial accident, the first woman was blind to the joy that was present, as most of us probably would be. We are culturally conditioned to focus on what is wrong and to look for the bad, which is part of the reason it can be difficult to find the good. We have to create new patterns in our thinking to shift attention to what's right, and this takes intentional effort and practice. It also takes the belief that there is a good story in there somewhere. The exercises help us do this by redirecting our attention to the positive aspects of our lives as we bump up against our old negative patterns and the prevailing cultural norms of doom and gloom.

Because it is such an important point, I'd like to share one more story about how we can find whatever we want in any situation. A while back during one of the presidential election campaigns, my husband and I felt very strongly about opposing candidates. We kept trying to convince each other why our particular candidate was the better choice, but we couldn't seem to get anywhere with it. It came time for the debates, and I could hardly wait.

The evening of the first debate finally arrived, and he and I eagerly propped ourselves up in front of the television. We sat there through the whole thing, listening intently. I could hardly contain my excitement throughout, since my candidate was clearly winning.

When the debate was finally over, I did not want to humiliate him any further, so I gently said, "Gee—it looks like my candidate won—huh?" He looked back at me like I had two heads and said, "What do you mean? *My* candidate clearly won that debate!" I glared at him, mortified. "What!" I said. "Were you not watching? *My* candidate won!" He lashed back, and so it went. I finally quit talking and just sat there with my face all scrunched up. What the heck had just happened?

What happened was the Poetic Principle in action. We each were looking for what we wanted to see in our candidate, and what we did not want to see in the other. And guess what? We found it! It was all there, and we each found what we were looking for. And the more debates we watched and the more articles we read, the more evidence we gathered to support our position. And when you gather enough evidence on any topic, it eventually becomes your truth.

In *Stumbling on Happiness*, Harvard Professor Daniel Gilbert summarizes the research on this concept beautifully:

> *When Dartmouth and Princeton students see the same football game, both sets of students claim that the facts clearly show that the other school's team was responsible for the unsportsmanlike conduct. When Democrats and Republicans see the same presidential debate on television, both sets of viewers claim that the facts clearly show that their candidate was the winner. When pro-Israeli and pro-Arab viewers see identical samples of Middle East news coverage, both proponents claim that the facts clearly show that the press was biased against*

their side. Alas, the only things these facts clearly show is that people tend to see what they want to see.[9]

For good or ill, we are subjective creatures. We shape our entire lives around what we *think* we see, but the fact is we see what we want to see. Our beliefs and thinking patterns direct our attention toward what we believe is important or enjoyable or interesting to pay attention to, and this process is not going to change anytime soon. The point is to be aware that we are all biased by nature, and that our perspective is just that: one perspective. We need to hold our beliefs and truths open to new information and further investigation.

The upside of accepting how biased we are is to realize that we have blind spots around joy. There is incredible beauty, love, grace, wisdom, opportunity, and possibility in every second and every person that we have not been able to see yet. Once we know there are all these wonderful things present in every moment that we have been filtering out, we can *choose* to find them. The more we look, the more we find, and that's when the joy really beings to grow.

The key to all of this is looking for what you want, which can be trickier than it first appears. Suppose right now I tell you *not* to think about the ocean. Do not put a single thought in your head about that large body of water, or the waves, or the seagulls or sand or seashells or any part of it. Whatever you do, do not think about the ocean. Good luck on that one, right?

Of course you had an image of the ocean in your mind. You cannot focus on the absence or the negative or the stopping or the "not" of something. Your mind does not hear the negative part and you actually end up putting attention on this very thing. There is a saying that what we resist, persists. This is how it works. The more you try to not think about something, or stop something, or fight against something, the more of it you actually bring into your awareness.

We have to get clear about what we want *more of* in order to create it and not *less of*. This is crucial to learning to use the power of focus effectively. It can be a difficult shift because we are so culturally programmed to focus on what we don't want. We are not nearly as clear about the things we like as we are about the things we don't like. This is the case for just about everything, including joy.

I was surprised to realize the degree most of us don't really know what makes us happy, myself included. You cannot look for the things that make you happy unless you know what they are. One of the first things people came to realize in doing the exercises is that they had misconceptions about joy. We've all heard the adage that joy is found in the simple moments, but I'm afraid to suggest that most of us don't really believe it. As astute as we like to think we are, we have all bought into some version of the ideal images we are presented in the media. And those images tend to be big and exciting.

Think about it for a moment. The joyful stories we see in the movies and news shows generally show some version of people acting heroically, overcoming major challenges, or getting acknowledged for some good "big" deed. Advertisers lure us further into the ideal with superbly decorated homes, nostalgic family gatherings, luxury cars, and gleaming white teeth. We are so bombarded with these glamorous images that we come to think happiness lies only in peak experiences, exceptional products, and perfect moments. But what about all the stuff in between?

That's where the real gems of life hide: in the proverbial journey. We tend to be blind to the possibilities for joy in the small moments because we are culturally conditioned to look for them in the big ones. This is something most of us have heard about and are aware of, at least on a cognitive level. The people in the study finally got it by doing the exercises. Here's how one woman described it:

> I learned that joy doesn't have to be big. Joy can be found in small, daily things. I found joy in floating in a lake with tiny dragonflies landing on my arms. I found joy in having something super-yummy planned for dinner, or cuddling with my three-year-old. How blessed I am!

Imagine watching a movie clip capturing the woman on the lake with the dragonflies. The camera zooms in and there she is, just floating on a lake. She's probably not wearing a designer bathing suit, and I bet she doesn't look like Barbie. She's not speaking or singing or sipping on a drink with an umbrella. As a matter of fact, if you had to describe the look on her face, it would be a toss-up between boredom and quiet content. She's just floating aimlessly. But wait—here comes a dragonfly! What will happen next? My gosh—it's landing on her bare arm! Look at it just sitting there, glistening a vibrant blue-green—as if stopping for a chat. Hold on—here come two more! They simultaneously dance upon her other arm as the first one takes off and begins circling...

Yes. This is a story of joy. Not the kind you will typically see portrayed in the movies or on TV, but the kind you will discover that sits hidden in every moment. It's not fancy, it's not exciting to watch, and it doesn't make the news. But believe it or not, this is what we're all searching for. It's learning to find the beauty and wonder that is present in every moment, especially the small ones that make up 99 percent of our life experience. It is being like a child, open to the wonder of each moment as if it were being experienced for the very first time. Here is how it showed up for several other participants:

> I forgot that I really enjoy tucking my daughter into bed at night. It was a chore I did so I could get on to the next one as quickly as possible. She won't be a little girl forever, and I'm glad I now remember how precious these moments are to me.

> I really appreciate nature and the people close to me. It was not a surprise, but I am surprised by the degree I am appreciative of them. I also realize it is nurturing and nourishing to bring these special aspects of my life to the forefront more often.

> I found that it gave me joy to reach out to someone else. To give them something they need. Find someone worse off and give to them.

> Because I really had to explore what "joy" meant to me, I learned a whole lot about the things that help me to feel joy, like an intimate connection with someone—my cats especially!— being outside, music, being kind and loving toward myself.

Consider the simplicity of what brought joy—tucking a child into bed, nature, close relationships, being of service, cats, and music. You potentially could experience any one of these on any given day. No one mentioned prestigious jobs, fancy cars, or exotic vacations. The longer people did the exercises, the clearer they got about what *really* brought them joy and not what they *thought* would bring them joy. Doing the exercises slowly debunked the myths people had about happiness and helped them discover where it really lived.

I'm laughing as I write this because I'm aware of one of my own myths I've been carrying for years after seeing the movie *Something's Gotta Give,* with Diane Keaton and Jack Nicholson. In the movie Diane Keaton is a successful writer working on her latest book in a multimillion dollar beach house that is to die for. I remember one scene in particular where she takes a break from writing and saunters into her gorgeous sunlit kitchen to get a bite of something I imagined to be pâté. Her clothes seem to meld and flow with the decor as she passes from one meticulously decorated room to another, and I remember romanticizing about how wonderful it would be to become an author. Not to mention the beach house.

So here I am several years later, living the dream. It's Saturday afternoon, and I'm typing away on my laptop in our nondescript, four-bedroom, colonial, middle-class cul-de-sac home. I'm sitting on a big green exercise ball as I work, which keeps my toes from going numb, and which I pretend counts as ab exercise. It's a luxury to be working in the den, since I typically get relegated to the family room while Jon's job with health insurance claims this space. He's busy putting up Christmas decorations and, rather than taking a break for pâté, I take a break to hold the ladder so he can hang big red bows outside our windows. I'm in my cozy sweatpants and an old faded T-shirt I bought in Lithuania fifteen years ago, topped off with my favorite moth-holed blue sweatshirt I confiscated from Jon a while back. I'm not sure what the kids are doing, but hopefully he's on top of that.

As pathetic as I may look, I honestly have to tell you I couldn't be happier in this moment. The part they don't show in the movie is the joy of birthing a new idea on paper. It's not very interesting to watch, but it fills my soul in a way nothing else can. I'm frankly unaware of my clothes and surroundings, and am completely engulfed in the unfolding of the words. As it turns out, the parts of this experience I thought would bring the most joy don't matter, and I completely missed the ones that do. I was blind to the unimaginable joy of creation.

Once we discover the things that really do bring joy, we can begin focusing on them to create more happiness. The first exercise—creating an appreciation list—is one of the best ways to do this, and the following story from one participant is a powerful example of how effective this exercise can be:

I was diagnosed after about ten years of chronic pain and chasing one "miracle cure" after another, with fibromyalgia and migraines. I'm still searching for the right combination of treatments, and add to that perimenopausal hormone fluctuations and you can imagine the basket case my husband came home to. Some nights I wondered why he came home at all.

Anyway, in my mind, there is no doubt that the exercises were the seeds that germinated into the harvest of well-being I feel today. When I started actively looking for those little things for which to feel grateful I found even greater things, and with that came clearer thinking. And I became a better health advocate for myself.

Now I'm getting up at 5:30 a.m. once again to exercise with my husband and I'm not taking afternoon naps because I'm not tired. And I'm amazed when it's 6 p.m. because the day has just seemed to slip by.

As an example of little things I felt grateful for in the beginning, I offer an excerpt from my journal:

July 19, 2006
I am grateful for hand lotion.
I am grateful for heating pads.
I am grateful for soap.
You said we really had to feel grateful for these things. Imagine life without soap. Imagine your back in so much pain you could hardly move and no heating pad. My husband said it best this morning when we were talking it over: "It's like a spiral of well-being from the seeds of gratitude."

Notice how simple the things were that brought her joy. Hand lotion, heating pads, and soap. As she focused on what she was grateful for, the good things began to grow, and her entire experience responded to her change in thinking. This again is the idea that you can find whatever you look for, which then becomes a bigger part of your experience.

There is an unspoken piece in all this: If you want to shift your focus to create more joy, whether in the small moments or the big ones, you have to take an active role in making it happen. It is a choice, and not something that just happens on its own. A study participant explains:

The most important thing I learned is that when it comes down to my personal joy, it may come from very unexpected

*places. It's not just about getting enough sleep and a break. Joy
is a more proactive state. There's a choice-fullness about it. For
me, it's not about going to it but choosing it and investing in it.
There's a personal investment in joy.*

I love how she discovered that *it's not about going to it but choosing
it and investing in it.* She is touching on an important distinction:
Focusing on joy is a choice. It is something we have to deliberately
choose to do; it is not a passive result of whatever happens to us.
We have to choose to look for the good in a situation or it won't
happen. We need to take an active role in creating our own happiness. Each day we need to make it a priority. Each day we need to
choose it again, as the following participant discovered:

> *A key learning for me was that joy is a choice. . . . I can
> choose my perspective. I choose it. I choose happiness. I claim it.*

Intentionally creating more joy is like making any other change
in our lives, whether it's a slimmer waistline or political reform.
We have to focus more attention on whatever it is we want more
of. This means putting happiness first.

I mentioned this earlier, as it is a key point Barry Neil
Kaufman discusses in his book *Happiness Is a Choice.* We need to
hold joy as our first priority and then go from there. When you
base your decisions and actions on what will bring you the most
happiness, you create jobs and relationships and experiences
that actually do make you happier. It's an internal prioritization
process. Putting happiness first may not sound all that different on the surface, but you'll find it makes all the difference in
the world. And I have the study results to prove it.

Putting joy first is the key to creating it, but it is a completely countercultural concept. In fact, it is seen as hedonistic in many circles, and "spiritually unenlightened" in others. Yet joy is what we ultimately seek as we make our major life decisions, whether it's choosing a mate or finding our calling. When you begin by intending to find joy and then live from that place, it changes your entire perspective, which changes your decisions—which changes your life. You have to put joy first in order to find it.

That's essentially what the exercises do. They compel you to look for what's right with your world, which builds new thought patterns in that direction. Once you find your true source of joy and stop chasing the proverbial pots of gold that lie in our cultural myths, you begin to see rainbows all around. By choosing to find the beauty and magnificence in every moment, you can save years (perhaps even a lifetime) of wasted effort looking elsewhere. Then you'll begin to experience the kind of joy that is beyond words, and you'll realize it was right there in front of you all along. Only now you can finally see it.

4

III. The Simultaneity Principle: Harness the Power of Questions

The one most impactful insight from the study was the thought that I truly do create my reality based on the questions I ask myself and the answers I think to those questions. I am in control of my happiness, and asking the right questions makes all the difference in the world.
—Study participant

The third principle in Appreciative Inquiry is the Simultaneity Principle. It suggests that change begins simultaneously in the moment we ask a question, so the questions we ask are really important. They instantly focus our thinking in one direction over another, so asking questions is one of the most powerful tools we have for making deliberate changes in our lives.

Let me show you how this works. Right now, I'd like you to take a minute to reflect briefly on the rest of your day today and what you will be doing. If it's late in the evening, you may want to think about tomorrow. Quickly review the various tasks and activities you'll be engaged in, the people you'll interact with, and your general state of affairs. The thoughts currently running through your head are indicative of the way you normally think about the future.

Now answer this question: "As you reflect on your day ahead, what is one thing you could do, no matter how small, that would increase your joy?" Think about it for a moment. It can be anything. Perhaps you could grab a warm cup of coffee on your way to work, take a few extra minutes to pet your cat, tell someone you love them, watch the sunset, take a few extra deep breaths, go walking at lunchtime, meet a friend for breakfast, take a nap, and so on. The point of this exercise is not for you to come up with a concrete answer, but for you to see how questions can direct your attention and shift your thinking in the moment they are asked. Rather than simply mulling over your day, you shift your attention to think about what would bring you joy. Participants found that asking this question over time caused them to do things differently, and to do different things.

Do you see how asking a question like this every day could reprioritize your thinking and bring happiness to the forefront? Can you imagine how it would gradually shift your focus to more of the things that bring you joy? As study participants found, asking this simple question can be a pivotal way of shifting your priority to begin living into joy each day.

Questions direct our attention, which in turn directs our experience. As we discussed in the Poetic Principle, whatever we focus on, grows. In order to create more joy we need to put more attention on it, and asking this question is one of the best ways to make that happen.

Let me give you another example of how this question initiates change as soon as it is asked. Suppose it's an average school day for me as a mother with two young children, and it's time for breakfast. Normally I would grab the cereal and milk and go about making lunches while they eat, with the unspoken goal of getting everyone out the door on time with the right notebooks, backpacks, lunches, notes, homework, show-and-tell items, box tops, library books, gloves, and I must be forgetting something!

Suppose instead, I spent a few minutes ahead of time asking myself what I could do to increase my joy that morning. Doing so would definitely change things for me both in that moment and going forward. I might decide to sit with my children while they eat and have a nice conversation. Perhaps I would have them pack their book bags before breakfast so getting out the door isn't so hectic. Over time I may decide to get up earlier so we are not so rushed and are more relaxed throughout the morning. The possibilities are endless, but the main idea is that I would do things differently and move toward joy if I asked myself this question.

Several stories about how asking this question initiated changes in people's live were shared. One woman had a particularly powerful experience:

> There was an exhibit in the city I really, really wanted to go to but our family could never quite work it out. It was the last week of the exhibit, and when I went to get tickets they were sold out. I sat down the second morning to do the joy exercises and decided that the one thing that would bring me joy that day would be to get into this exhibit. I didn't know if I had control over the outcome, but I said I would do everything to try and get in. I spent an hour or so trying to find ways to get tickets, but I

had no luck. I finally packed a backpack and just headed to the
exhibit. I made a large poster board that said I would pay $50
for a ticket, stood by the gate, and stared people down as they
went past. This is totally unlike me to do something like this! A
woman finally approached me who was leaving, and I was able
to get a ticket for only five dollars. It was the high point of my
entire summer, and I would have never done it if I had not been
doing the exercises.

Had this woman not asked the question, she would have missed
out on what she called "the high point of her entire summer." By
using the question to shift her focus she made a different choice
than she would have normally. And notice that her answer that
day was not a big thing such as buying a beach house or winning
the lottery. It was a ticket to a local event that created her peak
experience. Happiness really is in the small things. Here are two
additional ways the daily question helped study participants:

The daily question always forces me to focus and create
an intention for the day. That seems to set a container which I
live into. I imagine I'll continue this practice as an established
centering routine for my mornings.

There are times during the day I get overwhelmed and
stressed. The sentence from the morning is there in my head. I've
written it in the morning and I can quickly go back to it because
I wrote it that morning.

Asking this deliberate question shifts our attention simultaneously to joy, and our experience follows. You see, we are ask-

ing questions all day long without thinking about it. We have a whole series of habitual questions we ask from the moment we first open our eyes in the morning. It starts with things like "What day is it? What time is it? Should I get up now? When do I really have to get up? Can I just sleep ten more minutes? Do I really have to exercise today?" On and on our inner dialogue goes, directing our attention and experience in fairly predictable patterns that tend to create fairly consistent experiences. When we interject a new question, such as "What one thing can I do, no matter how small, to increase my joy?" it shifts the pattern. As we continue to ask the question a new thinking pattern eventually will form and the process will become automatic.

We can also use questions deliberately in our day-to-day interactions with others to shift our attention. This is a relatively advanced skill, but as you become more naturally appreciative you'll find yourself becoming aware of this possibility. Let me give you an idea of how it works.

Suppose I happen to sit next to you while watching a movie, and at the end we begin talking with each other. Since questions simultaneously direct attention in the moment they are asked, whoever asks the first question will drive the conversation. Suppose I start and say something like "Wow—that was a great movie. Aren't you glad we picked this one?" That will take the conversation in a positive direction. If you follow up with another question about what was fascinating, fun, or interesting about the movie, we will create an uplifting conversation together and feel good as we talk about it.

If instead I say, "Wow! That was a great movie. But don't you think the supporting actor did a lousy job?" If you agree and then follow up with a question on how the scenery could have

been better, too, we will take the conversation in a more negative direction. And remember, whatever we focus on, grows. The
longer we pick apart the movie the more we will find to dislike,
and we may determine it wasn't all that good in the end. I know
I've loved movies that have gotten bad ratings from the critics.
We obviously were looking for different things.

I'm not suggesting we alter the facts to make life look better
than we believe it is. If the movie was terrible, we can acknowledge
that and move on. What I'm suggesting is that we become more
aware of the direction our conversations are heading, and notice
that our questions are leading the way. If we ask questions about
what is wrong, broken, bad, painful, and so on, we can expect to
have a negative conversation and an experience to match. This is
not to say we should only talk about the good stuff and completely
ignore the negative aspects. I'm proposing we simply become
mindful of where our conversations are going so we can be more
attentive to where they end up. Rather than spending half an
hour ruminating in circles about how awful the movie was, we
can take five minutes to acknowledge whatever we need to say,
and then intentionally move the conversation in a more positive
direction toward what we want. One of the best ways we can shift
a conversation is with an appreciative question.

And what is an appreciative question, you ask? Let me tell
you another story. When my daughter was four she attended a
charming preschool with a wonderful outdoor play area. One
day she came home all upset, saying that one of the boys was
chasing her and making growling noises at her on the playground. In my daughter's story of what happened, based on her
past experiences and beliefs, growling was a bad thing. It made

her very upset. Had my son been the victim of the growler at the time, he probably would have enjoyed it thoroughly and growled right back.

But this was my daughter, and she came to me and wanted help. I wasn't sure what to do, so I decided to ask her a question that might help her frame the situation in a more positive way. My mind began scrambling for possibilities while she stood there, urgently waiting for an answer. In a panic, I rushed to think of something (anything!) to ask that would move her story in a more positive direction. So I stammered out the following uncertain question: "Gee, do you think he likes you and that's why he's growling at you? Do you think it's because he likes you?" Now I'll admit, it was hardly a profound question, but it was the best I could come up with at the time.

I'd like to tell you that my daughter responded instantly to the question and we had a lively discussion, but the fact is she simply stared up into the ceiling corner for the longest time. I could see the wheels spinning inside her head, but I had no clue where they were going. I actually got worried for a split second that I had said something really bad. What in the world was she thinking? I kept waiting for her to say something, but she never did. After a period of time she just walked away. I never heard any more about the growling.

About two weeks later my three-year-old son came home from preschool crying. He said that a boy had been hitting him and he wanted me to make him stop. Déjà-vu. The coincidence was not lost on me, so I decided to try the same thing. There was only one problem. I had a seriously conflicting story.

I did not know the growling boy, but I sure knew the hitting boy. I had seen him in action during drop-off and pickup, and it was not pretty. To suggest he was hitting my son because he liked him was ludicrous. What was I to do? It seemed preposterous to ask the question, but as my son stared at me with those desperate eyes, I decided to give it a try.

I said to him through clenched teeth and all the sincerity I could muster (which was about none), "Gee, do you think he likes you and that's why he's hitting you? Do you think it's because he likes you?" At that moment, all these mother alarms started going off in my head wondering things like "What the heck am I doing? What if this kid really whacks him good next time? Am I lying? Where is the mother manual for how to deal with these things?"

While ruminating on these possible disasters, I finally looked over at him and realized he was responding exactly like my daughter had. He was staring up into the corner of the ceiling and not saying a word: an eternity of silence for a three-year-old. Then he walked away. I never heard any more about the hitting.

The end of the school year came, and guess what? Both of my children ended up becoming best friends with these two boys. Not just good friends, but best friends. My daughter started playing the "growling game" on the playground and became inseparable from the growling boy. The "hitting boy" continued to hit other kids, but either did not hit my son any longer, or if he did hit him, it didn't bother him. Either way, they got along wonderfully and were able to turn a tenuous relationship into a joyful one.

I'm not suggesting in the least that this is how we should handle bully situations. I'm sharing this story to illustrate the power of questions to shift our experience, and how big a shift

we can make with small questions. Children have an especially easy time of reframing situations since they do not have
a long history of beliefs and assumptions to undo. My son could
go from bully to best friend in two days, but there was no way I
could make that leap. By the way, I tried this again with each of
them a few years later and it didn't work. They had too many stories of their own to undo by that time.

Consider the question I asked each of them: "Gee, do you
think he likes you?" If I were to write a book of the one hundred
most powerful questions in Appreciative Living, this question
probably would not make the cut. Yet look how powerful it was in
these situations. It significantly shifted an important relationship from being painful to joyful for each of my children.

You see, it's not about asking the right questions. *It's about
asking the questions that take us to the right places.* And what are
the right places? The right places are *any* place that is *better* than
the place we are in, even if it's just a little bit better. It's about
always moving our conversations and stories forward. That's
what makes an appreciative question.

In my imagined book of the most powerful questions you
could ask, do you know what would be at or near the top of the
list? It would be "What do I want *more of*?" Does this sound
familiar, from the Poetic Principle? It is a great question to ask
in any situation when you want to shift to an appreciative focus.
Let me show you one example of how to use this question.

Suppose I have a relative who likes to poke fun at me in a
mean way, and because of our family situation, I am forced to
spend a fair amount of time with him. I want to change this
dynamic because it ruins some of the family gatherings for me,
so I decide to remedy the situation by intentionally changing

my focus with a new question. Everything is present in every moment and situation, and I know if I look hard enough I can find some good in this and create another story that is more uplifting than the one I'm currently experiencing.

One of the first questions I can ask to try to initiate change is "What do I want more of in this situation?" Suppose I think about it and decide that I want him to stop making fun of me and others. In this case I am focused on what I want *less of*, and not *more of*. If you remember from the Poetic Principle, focusing on the negative of something actually redirects our attention to the very thing we want to rid ourselves of. If I focus on him not making fun of people, I will actually increase my experience of this unwanted behavior. What is it I want *more of*?

This is where it gets interesting. If you remember back to the Constructionist Principle, I discussed how we have full control over our own experience but no control over the experience of others. I illustrated that with a modified version of the serenity prayer, which bears repeating:

> Grant me the serenity to accept the people I cannot change,
> the courage to change the one I can,
> and the wisdom to know it's me.

While it's hard medicine to swallow, I cannot make this man do anything differently. Joy resides fully in my own thinking. So I have to focus on the *experience* that I want *more of* in the presence of him. That is completely within my power. What experience do I want to have as he does what he has always done, and will likely continue to do?

Suppose I dig in and realize that what I want is to feel good and stand in my power when he pokes fun at me. I can now ask a whole series of appreciative questions to get me there. Again, an appreciative question is any question that takes you to a place that is better than the one you were in. It's a question that helps you frame a situation in a slightly better way.

Here are some examples of appreciative questions that could be used in this situation. You could ask yourself just one, or you could systematically work through all of them for a thorough reframing. A summary of these questions is also provided for quick reference in Appendix D: Questions for Reframing Difficult Situations.

- What strengths does this man have, and what is good about him?
- What do I like about him?
- What do I stand to learn or gain from this?
- In what ways will my life be better after having worked through this?
- Who do I know who deals well with these types of situations, and what can I learn from him or her?
- When have I dealt successfully with a similar situation in the past, and what can I apply from that?
- What are my greatest strengths, and how can I use them to help me in this situation?
- What am I excited or curious about in all this?
- What are two good things that could possibly come out of this?
- What are three reasons why I'm glad this situation has come up?
- How does this situation make me appreciate other people in my life even more?

- How will the learning from this situation spill over into other areas of my life?
- What am I grateful for in all of this?

Can you feel how these types of questions not only take you to a better place, but help you deal successfully with what is going on? Do you see how they will help you get the same results as problem solving, but in an uplifting way? Do you notice yourself feeling more hopeful by simply reading through them? Appreciative questions open up new possibilities for creating more of what you want. Rather than looking at what is wrong and trying to fix it, you look at what is right and how you can make your experience better.

I know that shifting to a positive focus may sound radical, and it is. That's why it works so well. Before you get concerned that you have to give up your negative focus, let me ease your fears. You don't need to give up anything. I'm suggesting you *add* these questions into your current way of dealing with situations, and then you be the judge of what works best. There is a learning curve to this way of thinking, and the more you do it, the more comfortable you get and the more effective it becomes.

I know I keep reiterating this, but it is without a doubt the biggest area of misunderstanding in this work. Asking these appreciative questions does not mean you ignore the bad stuff. In the example above, I am well aware that I don't like the way my relative puts me down, and I am not ignoring this in any way. What I am doing is intentionally putting my focus and energy into what I want, which is to feel better about him and myself in the situation. I can only do this by shifting my attention to it. It feels very unnatural at first, but with lots of practice it eventually can feel normal. On my website www.Appreciative Living.com, I list other appreciative questions you can ask to create more of what you want in areas such as health, career, relationships, and dating. Asking questions is an incredibly powerful way to initiate change in any area of your life.

Narrative therapist Michael Hoyt says, "All questions are leading questions." All questions take us somewhere, even if it's simply back to reinforce what we already believe. We can use appreciative questions to shift our experiences and open up whole new possibilities in our blind spots to joy.

The next time you are in a conversation with yourself or someone else, think about the direction your questions are taking you. There are only two possibilities: upward or downward. When in doubt, you can always fall back on one simple question: *What experience do I want more of?* It may not be the perfect question, but it will move you in the right direction.

5

IV. The Anticipatory Principle: Act from Inspiration Rather Than Desperation

Visioning takes you into a whole new path.
It clears the day-to-day clutter.
—*Study participant*

The fourth principle in Appreciative Inquiry is the Anticipatory Principle. It suggests that the images we anticipate in our minds about the future can influence the future we actually experience. It's almost like we are walking around with crystal balls in our heads, and we can look up into them to see what's coming. Better yet, we can intentionally plant images of what we want in order to make it happen.

At any given time, we all have pictures in our minds of what we anticipate the future will bring, whether we are aware of it or not. Let me show you what I mean. Right now, very briefly think about what will be going on for you next month. Picture what kinds of experiences you will be having and how you expect to feel through it all. Consider how you expect the month to unfold and imagine yourself going through the motions as if you were watching a movie. Now estimate how good you expect this month to be on a scale of one to ten, with one being horrible, five being neutral, and ten being absolutely phenomenal.

The scenes you just imagined about next month and the number you picked are fateful. In other words, if you pictured a great month and gave it a high rating, you are more likely to have a good experience. Unfortunately, it also works in the other direction. The way things turn out has a lot to do with what we expect, and we can learn to use this to our advantage. Rather than simply acting out the unconscious images we hold, we can become aware of and deliberately work with the pictures we have in our heads.

Another word for leveraging the power of our imagination is visualization, which essentially is the process of intentionally creating images in our minds of what we want most in order to help make it happen. Athletes often work with visualization, and it is now a common practice for many people. Many studies in a variety of sports validate the practice of visualization. Rosalene Glickman, in *Optimal Thinking*, provides this example:

> One group practiced basketball every day, the second mentally visualized themselves practicing, and the third—the control group—did neither. The study found that the men who physically practiced and those who mentally practiced were equally good on the court. The control group lost to both groups.[10]

Multiple studies have shown that imagining ourselves exercising or practicing a new skill can be as effective as actually doing it. One of my favorite books that talks about this, as well as the latest developments in brain science, is *The Brain That Changes*

Itself by psychiatrist and psychoanalyst Norman Doidge. In this reader-friendly book, Doidge describes the nature of imagination and action:

> *One reason we can change our brains simply by imagining is that, from a neuroscientific point of view, imagining an act and doing it are not as different as they sound. When people close their eyes and visualize a simple object, such as the letter* a, *the primary visual cortex lights up, just as it would if the subjects were actually looking at the letter* a. *Brain scans show that in action and imagination many of the same parts of the brain are activated. That is why visualizing can improve performance.*[11]

Many of us know intuitively that visualization works, but it is exciting to see the physiological evidence to back it up. In *Train Your Mind, Change Your Brain*, *Newsweek* science writer Sharon Begley cites recent studies on visualization, concluding that "merely thinking about playing the piano leads to a measureable, physical change in the brain's motor cortex, and thinking about thoughts in certain ways can restore mental health."[12] I believe we have only scratched the surface of what's possible with visualization, and it will be interesting to watch how we learn to leverage and maximize this fascinating tool.

We can use visualization to imagine anything we desire in our lives, but the trick is often in figuring out what we want. As I've mentioned before, we are so culturally programmed to focus on what we don't want that many of us don't know what we do want. I covered this in the previous principles; it is important to get clear about what we want more of in order to create it. The same is true with visualization.

When participants in the study visualized their ideal joy-filled life once a week, it helped them begin to get clear about what they wanted most in their lives. For several people this was a tremendously valuable insight:

> *The weekly visioning helped me clarify exactly what I wanted in my life . . . or at the very least, to see where I was clear about what I wanted and where I was not.*

> *The exercise of visioning my desired future helped me get clear on what I want in my life . . . I plan to repeat the exercise with my husband and family to see what we want to build together—and maybe they will open up my vision a little too.*

> *I learned that my ideal life is not as solidified in my mind as I thought it was. By having to write it four different times, I realized that I need to get a little more clarity . . . Writing this down made that clearer to me.*

Many of us don't even realize that we lack clarity about what we want in our lives: It is one of those things you don't know that you don't know. By practicing the visioning exercise, participants realized they needed and wanted a better sense of where their lives were heading. One woman in particular had a powerful realization as a result:

> *I looked forward to the visioning exercises all week. Prior to beginning the study, my long-term goals ended just a few years in the future and I wasn't sure where I wanted my life to go after that. This made me pretty nervous, but through a combination*

of the exercises and some "fateful" events that happened, I now feel very confident that I have figured out my life's direction for the next few decades. I started seeing indications that it was working a few weeks after the study, and things started to manifest. So many synchronicities began and now I am going back to school to completely change careers in the fall. I hope to keep doing those once-a-week visions to help keep me on track and hopeful about the changes I want to manifest in my life and the world.

As this woman became clear about what she really wanted in the future, it all came together rather quickly, and now she is in school preparing for a new career. Again, I find that for many people the hardest part is figuring out what they want. The actions we need to take to reach our dreams become pretty clear once we figure out where we want to go. It's that first part that's tricky, and it is why many of us seem to have trouble getting off square one.

Here's a little secret about the practice of visualization—you're already doing it. That's right. You do it every day, and you've been doing it all your life. When I asked you earlier to think about next month, you had to visualize it. When you begin your day and start to think about what you will be doing so you can pick out the appropriate clothes, you are visualizing. Anytime you think about the future and picture what might happen, you are visualizing. The question is, how are those images getting up there?

If you are like the average person, the short answer is that someone else is putting them there. The pictures you hold of your future are like a giant melting pot of all the conversations, interactions, influences, and experiences of all the people, media, institutions, cultures, animals, plants, and just about anything else you can think of with which you have come in contact. Going back to the Constructionist Principle, remember that the meaning we make has a lot to do with the company we keep.

Let's take a simple example. Suppose I ask you to think about what you would like to do this weekend. As you can imagine, there will be as many answers to this as there are people reading this book. But consider how your answer is affected by the following:

- What your friends and family like to do
- Where you live
- What you were raised to believe about weekends
- What responsibilities you have at home and work
- What neighbors and other people around you do
- What your religious beliefs and personal values suggest you do
- What the media says you should do
- What your financial status is, and what other people in your financial situation do

There are an infinite number of influences, but the point is that you don't decide what you want in isolation. If you don't make time to intentionally think about your future, the media and your family and friends will be happy to fill in the blanks. In other words, it's not really your life you're living: it's theirs. And they will be happy to continue to influence you until you take back the reins. So while it is about impossible not to be influenced by others, you can at least get in the driver's seat and become conscious of where the bus is heading. That's exactly what visualization does for us: It puts us back in control of our lives.

One interesting thing that happens when you begin to imagine the ideal and get in touch with your dreams is you begin to question the limits you have always assumed were there. You don't even realize you live within these limits until you brush up against them in visioning. It's not until you create a picture of your ideal future that you start to step back and say, "Is this possible? Do I really believe I can create this kind of life? Am I thinking too big? Or am I not thinking big enough?" And then the fun begins.

You get to question everything you've been told about what is possible and everything you believe. This really is a good thing if you choose to follow the proverbial rabbit hole. If you dive in to your story of the future, you'll come to see that most, if not all, of your limits are self-imposed. It may take a while to get there (it took me several years of intense work), but eventually you come to see that the only thing standing in your way is your thinking.

Now we're back to the Constructionist Principle, where we live in the world our stories create. It turns out we exist in a self-imposed box of limits. As independent scholar and leadership adviser Robert Cooper says in *Get Out of Your Own Way*:

> It's as if you've been working endlessly and diligently to
> polish the walls, floors, and furniture of a small room, always
> believing that this is the room of life. But once you've seen today's
> good and great for the constraints they are, then a secret window
> gets opened, and all at once you realize that you've been missing

the big picture—that this is only one small closed room in a vast
city, country, planet, and universe. Everything begins to change.[13]

The only thing keeping us from creating whatever we want in
our lives is our limiting beliefs. And do you know which are the
most limiting beliefs? The answer surprised me. I had always
thought it was our negative beliefs, such as, "I'm not good
enough," or "I'm not smart enough," but, in fact, David Cooperrider suggests that it is our beliefs of what's possible that are
most limiting.[14] So the question is: "What do you believe is possible in your life? What is the absolute most amount of money
you think you could make next year? What is the absolute best
relationship you can imagine ever having with your mother-
in-law? Your teenager? How joyful do you really believe you can
get?" This is the box within which you live, and your life will not
move beyond it.

Believe it or not, this is also good news. Do you know why?
You are the one who created the limits, so you are the one who
can change them. And guess what is one of the most effective
ways of blowing past limiting beliefs? Visualization! When we
deliberately imagine the ideal, we give ourselves permission to
think outside the proverbial box. As we go on a mental exploration of what our perfect, beautiful, ideal life looks and feels like,
we begin to break down beliefs we have that say it isn't possible.
Believe me, it is a skill worth developing.

While all of us know how to visualize unconsciously, visualizing intentionally is a skill. But it is one we can all learn and,
while it can be hard for some at first, it does get easier with practice. It can be as simple as taking fifteen seconds before a meeting to get clear about your intention and imagine how you want

the meeting to go, or as detailed as taking an hour to formally describe and write about every aspect of your ideal life. We can use visualization to create anything we want. In chapter 10, I will give an in-depth explanation of the visualization process.

An interesting thing happens when we begin to visualize to create our ideal future: We find our real power. As we get in touch with our dreams, we become inspired to act on them and make significant changes in our lives. Here is one man's story:

> *I have to say that although these six months have been a roller-coaster ride for me in some parts of my life, participating in this exercise has kept my spirits higher and my joy greater than I would have ever expected under the circumstances.*
>
> *I had been having excruciating problems at work with a new administration. The negative style has turned a largely happy institution into one where morale is down, people are leaving, and many are just plain going through the motions. It's a very sad situation.*
>
> *While focusing on my joy over the last six months, I have come to the realization that I no longer "need" to stay with this employer. I think that the daily reflection on what brings me joy helped me to see that the joy that I once found in my work experience is no longer there for me. It helped me make a simple promise to myself each day to do something to increase my joy. In a very small way (that turned out to be very large), the exercise got me to consciously focus on my level of joy and to make a commitment to do something about it.*
>
> *I am now in my last few days of work at this institution. I will leave at the end of the month, and I am delighted by the prospects. I no longer need to live in an environment that does*

not bring out the best in me. I DO NEED TO FOCUS ON A JOYFUL LIFE.

Joy abounds if you take steps to look for it and make it a powerful force in your life. Thank you for bringing this exercise to me in this very critical moment in my life!!!

This is a great story for a lot of reasons, one being that it helps illustrate a couple of big cultural myths that surround joy. The first myth is that love/joy/happiness is blind. We think that getting happier puts us in la-la land. We tend to believe that the only way to see the good is to ignore the bad, but this is not the case at all. Focusing on what's good is something you do in addition to whatever else you want to pay attention to. It's not an either/or; it's a both/and. We think that focusing on joy means burying our head in the sand and doing our best to look away from the things we don't want to see. This is not appreciative thinking; it is denial.

Consider the story above. The man in this situation started focusing on what was good about the company and situation, which in no way blinded him to the reality of what was going on. In fact, my experience says that the opposite is true. The better we feel about a situation the more we are able to see. Pain and fear tend to make us run away and hide from things we don't want to acknowledge. As positive psychology researcher Sonja Lyubomirsky reports in *The How of Happiness*:

> *Research shows that optimists are more, not less vigilant of risks and threats (they don't have their blinders on), and optimists are very much aware that positive outcomes are dependent on their efforts (they don't wait around for good things to happen).*[15]

Lyubomirsky points out a second myth this story also dispels: that if you start feeling good about a situation and you start appreciating everyone around you, then you won't take any action to change anything. Why would you? You're not in any pain, and you're not angry about what's going on, so why would you cause a stir? We think anger and fear are the only things that motivate us to change. Do you know why we think this? Because there are people all around us doing it every day! Turn on the television, read the newspaper, look around, and you'll see it. We are so culturally conditioned to act from negative emotion that we don't even know it's possible to do it any other way. But let's take a look at what it means to act from fear and anger.

If you think about it, fear tends to immobilize us at first. I don't want to dwell on this too much because we're here to talk about joy, but I want to make a point. Think about what you do when you are afraid. Isn't your first reaction to recoil and pull back? Can you feel how vulnerable and insecure this place is? Fear can actually keep us stuck until it gets so bad we finally react out of it.

And then there's anger. What happens when you get really mad? While it's different for each of us, it usually involves action of some kind, but not necessarily the best kind. Screaming, ranting, raving, and violence are all associated with angry actions. I know that some of my biggest regrets took place when I acted out of anger.

There's a whole other range of negative emotions, but the point is that action that comes from a place of feeling bad generally leads to more of the same. Yet many of us are so accustomed to acting from negative emotion that we are skeptical of acting from a place of feeling good. Frankly, we're not even sure what it looks like.

But it turns out that joy acts, too. And guess what? When we act from a place of joy, our actions are effective. They are uplifting. They make sense. They are in our best interest. And you know what else? They are powerful. You know this intuitively. Think Dr. Martin Luther King Jr., Mahatma Gandhi, and Mother Teresa. There is a quote by Marianne Williamson from *A Return to Love* that we've all seen, but I still love it no matter how many times I read it:

> *Our deepest fear is not that we are inadequate. Our deepest fear is that we are powerful beyond measure. It is our light, not our darkness, that most frightens us. We ask ourselves, Who am I to be brilliant, gorgeous, talented, fabulous? Actually, who are you not to be? You are a child of God. Your playing small doesn't serve the world. There's nothing enlightened about shrinking so that other people won't feel insecure around you. We are all meant to shine, as children do. We were born to make manifest the glory of God that is within us. It's not just in some of us; it's in everyone. And as we let our own light shine, we unconsciously give other people permission to do the same. As we're liberated from our own fear, our presence automatically liberates others.[16]*

The relationship between joy and power is not just happy talk. There is plenty of research that shows the better we feel the better we think.[17] When we experience positive emotion, our thinking becomes more expansive.[18] We are more creative and better at problem solving, solution generation, and decision making.

The opposite is also true. When we are sad or frightened our thinking contracts, and we are limited in our ability to function cognitively. It's a myth that we need to feel bad in order to make change. Negative emotion inhibits our ability to act wisely, and our cognitive ability to determine the right actions. Actions that we take while feeling angry or frustrated tend to be reactions and are not well thought through. We are instinctively reacting out of pain, rather than taking inspired action in a meaningful way. It is the difference between moving from what we want and moving toward what we do.

Think about what the man in the story a few pages back wrote: "Doing the exercises has kept my spirits higher and my joy greater than I would have ever expected under the circumstances." The exercises helped him feel better about a difficult situation and allowed him to experience greater happiness even though times were tough. And then he says, "They helped me to see that the joy I once found in my work is no longer there…and to make a commitment to do something about it." Making joy the priority inspired him to take action. Notice he did not say, "Oh now that I'm feeling better, I'll just camp out in this organization for the next thirty years." Because he started feeling so good, he could *not* stay in the organization any longer. As he felt better and paid more attention to his happiness, he realized he needed to make a change. He had been with this company for years prior to the study, and the current situation had been going on for months. He had thoughts of leaving before, but it wasn't until he became more joyful that he took action. This is an example of acting from a place of feeling good. It also illustrates the idea that when we put joy first, we make choices that align our jobs and everything else to help create that joy.

Let me clarify: I am not suggesting here that if you don't enjoy your job, you should leave! What I'm trying to show is that feeling good can inspire you into action; it does not make you the least bit passive. If you do not enjoy your job, there are a whole host of actions other than leaving that you can take to feel better. But until you feel better about the situation you can be blind to a lot of them.

Consider the example in the last chapter of the woman who went out by herself to solicit event tickets. She had never done anything like this before, and the decision to do so came out of her choice to put joy first. In her book *Loving What Is*, Byron Katie talks about the myth that fear is what motivates us to act. She writes:

> *A question I often hear is, "If . . . I'm no longer fearful for the planet's welfare, why would I get involved in social action? If I felt completely peaceful, why would I bother taking action at all?" My answer is "Because that's what love does."*
>
> *The fear of not being fearful is one of the biggest stumbling blocks for people beginning inquiry. They believe that without stress, without anger, they wouldn't act, they would just sit around with drool running down their chins. Whoever left the impression that peace isn't active has never known peace the way I know it. I am entirely motivated without anger. The truth sets us free, and freedom acts.*[19]

The clarity and centering that comes from joy is powerful. When we visualize what we want we tap into our source of joy and become inspired to take action. The changes that come from this place of inspiration are much more effective and powerful than the changes we make from fear or anger. You can intuitively sense the difference. In the past I spent a lot of my life acting from anger, so I know firsthand what kind of results that space creates. Speaking of which, let me share a story that shows the kind of results you get from anger rather than inspiration.

In the early 1990s, I took a new engineering job, and when I started work I found out they had a golf league. I was excited to get on it, but there was one little problem: It was a men's league. I ignored the fact it was a men's league and began asking team captains if I could join their team. They sort of shuffled around uncomfortably when I asked and mumbled various politically correct versions of no. Each rejection was like fuel on my internal fire, and I became more determined to get on the league.

I went to the next officers' meeting to plead my case, and they very nicely pulled out the bylaws. We could not find an explicit statement saying women could not play on the league, so they could not officially keep me off. Since no one would let me play on their team, I decided I would create a new team in the league. And I did.

I found three men who had wanted to play for some time but couldn't get on the league for a variety of reasons. We officially formed a new team we called the Sandbaggers, and I started feeling victorious. I thought I had won the war, but some of the battalions did not get the message that it was over.

I'll never forget the first evening we played. You could never make a movie of it because it would look too staged. I can't remember exactly how it went, but when it was time to start I was up first. I had never played on a league in my life and had no clue what I was doing. I walked up to the tee box stunned and terrified. I turned to my right and looked to see fifteen men standing in a straight line in complete silence, all staring straight at me. I thought I was going to pass out. "Perfect," I thought, "a firing squad."

And then it got worse. I realized at that moment that I didn't know where to go. Should I hit from the men's tee box or the women's? I didn't know who to ask, so I shot a general half-question to the lineup. Complete silence—fifteen deadpan faces staring back. I decided to hit from the men's tee box so no one could complain later that I was getting an unfair advantage. I finally addressed the ball with shaky hands and began to slowly pull my club back to swing when one of the men in the gallery screamed, "Why don't you go hit from the wussie tees where you belong?" Those were his exact words. They etched themselves on my brain on that very painful day.

I tried to be brave, and so I turned to the lineup and said something very small and weak in a little piglet voice, and then prayed to God and every being I could think of to please, please not let me cry right now. I turned back to the ball and made a deal with the universe that if I could just hit this thing, I would never do anything this stupid again for the rest of my life. It's probably good I did not have to follow through on my promise.

I raised my club and swung as hard as a frazzled person could and I whacked the heck out of the ball. The only trouble was I also sliced it badly, which meant it took off in a hard right direction. There was a big fence to the right, and after smacking it squarely, the ball dropped down, rolled, and stopped about twenty-four inches from the women's tee box. To this day, I can't think of any way the situation could have been more humiliating, other than if I had ripped my pants. I proceeded to duff the ball all the way to the green, wondering what in the world I was thinking when I got myself into this mess.

Believe it or not, the story does have a happy ending. That first outing was a nightmare, but it got much better after that. By the end of the season the men had pretty much accepted me, and I ended up having a lot of fun. The next year they officially opened the league to women, so you would call this a success story by current cultural standards.

It is also a story of how things tend to go when you work from anger. Change happens, but it can create a lot of mess and pain for everyone involved. The impact also tends to be minimal. Anger blocks effective thinking and creates a lot of resistance, and this combination really slows down progress. In this case, it took almost a year of struggle and manipulation to allow women to golf in this particular league. I don't think a single woman joined that first year, which tells you just how important this "milestone" was in the scheme of things. While I could claim victory in the end, I'm not sure it justified the effort.

Acting from anger, fear, pain, and other negative emotions is so culturally pervasive that we don't even question it. We see people "fighting" for this and that, with the belief that anger is an effective fuel for their cause. And it is fueling the cause, but I would question the effective part. It does create change and sometimes it is very good change. But I'd like to suggest that there's a better way.

Acting from joy is a whole different ball game. It uses the energy of inspiration rather than exasperation and desperation. When we are inspired we can move mountains, and visualization shifts us into this place of power. My work with Appreciative Living comes from this place, and I'm continually amazed at the impact it is having. I do more from joy now than I ever did from fear and anger.

The third visualization exercise helps us find our real power and create positive, powerful change. It is an incredible tool for creating inspired action and moving beyond our limiting beliefs. To quote Antoine de Saint-Exupéry: "If you want to build a ship, don't drum up the people to gather wood, divide the work, and give orders. Instead, teach them to yearn for the vast and endless sea."

What do you yearn for? Which dreams burn deep within your soul and long for the light of day? Dare to raise them up into your thoughts and imagine them into being. The Anticipatory Principle suggests that this very practice will help them come true. Then prepare to be inspired beyond anything you've ever known, and go into the world and do what you love. At that point no one and nothing can stop your joy.

{ 6 }

V. The Positive Principle:
Be Upward Trendy

The dedicated focus on the positive became a way to "wake up" to
the good that is happening in the present . . . not longing for past
good things, or desperately hoping for future good things. Actually
recognizing, hey, this is a good thing right here and right now.
—*Study participant*

The last of the five Appreciative Inquiry principles is
the Positive Principle, which suggests that positive emotion
is essential for effective change. Creating more joy not only
feels good; it is central to living a productive life. We can build
momentum toward greater joy by focusing on the positive core
and paying attention to what really takes us upward.

The positive core refers to a belief that every organization, situation, or person contains a host of good things at the
core, such as wisdom, knowledge, successful strategies, positive attitudes, best practices, skills, resources, and capabili-
ties.[20] We know from the Poetic Principle that whatever we focus
on grows, and if we look hard enough for the positive core we
will find it and raise it up.

The more we focus on the positive core of ourselves and

others, the happier we become. It is a journey of discovery as we inquire into the best of who we are and what life has to offer. And make no mistake, finding the positive core and becoming happier is a journey. It can be hard at first to see the good, but the more we work with it the easier it gets:

I have this natural ability to magnify the horrible while always downplaying the good. The exercises helped me to even out my perspective. They kind of gave permission to experience and give some concentration to the bright side of life.

The morning exercises were like consciously choosing to put on a pair of glasses through which I could see my day differently. Noticing little things. The exercises kept the process of reflecting on my blessings in the forefront of my mind.

Doing the exercises is like the discipline of cleaning off your joy glasses. It doesn't take that much time to clean them off.

Finding what's right with ourselves and the world is a process, and it is as unique as each one of us is. You have to start from where you are and go from there. If you haven't spent a lot of time looking at your positive core, it can feel uncomfortable at first. But if you stay the course and continue to look, gradually you will begin to see the wonder around you. You will begin to discover what really makes you happy, not just what you think would make you happy.

The best way to discover what really brings you joy is to try something and notice whether it actually makes you happier or not. Does that sound too obvious? It really is that simple, but most of us don't take the time to drop in and reflect on our experience in this way. We don't often stop to consider how we actually feel when we engage in an activity. Here is what several people in the study discovered as they tried out some things and reflected on their experience:

> *At first I would think of one thing I could do today to increase my joy, which was walking, but after the first week I figured out that walking is not doing it for me. It brings me joy for that thirty minutes, but I wanted to know what quality will carry me through the day. I decided it was patience—to see things in a lighter way. Really, things are not all that serious.*

> *One thing I learned to do to increase my happiness was to accept my unhappiness. Don't fight it. Relax into it. Just be with it.*

> *I realized that at first you have to "clean out your house" to get to really creating joy. At first I thought that doing things like cleaning the dishes wasn't "spiritual enough" to increase my joy . . . it really does help you feel better to clean the kitchen or take care of that one thing that is bugging you.*

Notice the examples above range from developing patience and accepting unhappiness to cleaning the dishes. For someone in a lot of emotional strife, creating a little more joy may begin by finding ways to briefly relieve painful feelings. Or, as above, it may be in accepting the pain. It might be found in simply cleaning out a closet. We each have to find it out for ourselves, and that is why there is no universal prescription for joy. There is no one right way to do it. We are all in different places with varying needs, so we must begin from where we are.

Increasing joy is a gradual process of getting a little happier over time; it's not about going from hopelessness to enlightenment. In the above quotes, people found small ways to ease trying situations. They did not discover the perfect answer so they would never again get flustered when a difficult situation arose. They uncovered simple ways to ease their struggle. Increasing joy is about learning to make your everyday experiences gradually a little more pleasant. It is not about creating the perfect moment or the absolute best experience, but slowly improving your daily experiences.

I've been working on joy for some time now and still have a long way to go. At this stage I'm learning to breathe more deeply, to relax into and trust whatever life presents. Sometimes it works and I feel like I'm really making progress, and other times I get angry and flustered and wonder how the heck I can help anyone else when I can't even help myself. That's when I try to step back and look at the big picture and realize that overall I'm moving in a positive direction.

Let me give you an image to explain this idea further. In the two graphs that follow, I show an exaggerated difference between an average, "normal" life experience compared to what it might look like on the joy journey. Note that the purpose of these graphs is to compare the overall differences and not to give a realistic picture of the actual journey.

The first graph is my depiction of a normal life line of a person, which is jagged in shape like an irregular heartbeat. There are highs and lows in the journey, but the overall trend of the line is relatively flat.[21] The average happiness level does not change that much over time.

Normal Life

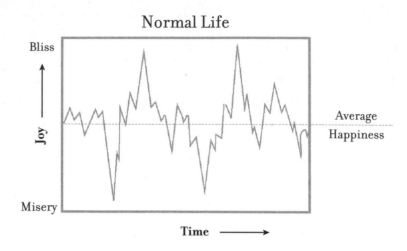

Joy Journey

Now consider the joy journey. The line is also jagged with ups and downs, but the overall trend is up. It looks more like a graph of the S&P 500 than an irregular heartbeat. There are still peaks and perhaps a depression along the way, but you see a gradual upward movement of the line over time. That is what the joy journey is about—creating an upward trend in happiness. It's slowly making the small moments just a little bit better. We never really do arrive, but it's a continual upward process.

If you look more closely, you'll see a second difference in the joy journey. There is a flattening of the line as well. In other words, as you go along the highs aren't quite so high and the lows aren't so low. As we learn to handle the bad situations better, they don't take us down as far or for as long as they did before. On the other end, the happy moments don't have as much novelty as before; we seem to acclimate to them. The more joy we have, the less of a surprise it is when it shows up again. It seems we become more emotionally stable. [22]

The best question to ask is not "Are you happy?" but "Are you getting happier overall? Is life getting a little more joyful in general? Are things going a little better?" That is what the joy journey is about, and that is how it works. All those tiny bits add up to big changes over time. When you have that bad day or week and feel like you are taking two steps backward, just know that is part of the path. There will still be down times, but if you stay the course and keep doing the exercises, eventually it will pay off. One day you'll have an experience that used to trip you up and you'll sail through it. At that moment you'll realize your life has jumped up a notch in overall happiness, and it is different in a significant way.

Along the joy journey, you realize that small or routine moments hold tremendous potential. It's because there are so many of them! Consider the types of activities we typically engage in: working, driving, sorting mail, paying bills, cleaning, putting things away, cooking, shopping, bathing, and caring for parents, pets, and children. These activities tend to consume most of our time, yet we tend to look toward the big milestones when thinking about significant life changes.

Consider for a moment how much time you will spend simply eating over the next week. What if you found a way to significantly increase your joy during mealtime? This one change would be realized many times over and could ultimately have an impact on your general sense of happiness. The opposite is also true. If you have ever gone on a diet you did not enjoy (is there any other kind?) you know how drastically it can cut into your overall happiness.

Do you see the potential in your simple daily activities? If you can learn to enjoy the scenery as you ride to work, or put some great music on while cleaning the house, or stop for a moment to really see your child—you've uncovered a gold mine! Learning to enjoy the small moments more is *not* a trivial investment of your efforts. It is one of the keys to creating an overall upward trend.

Now, I have to be honest. Even though I really get the idea that increasing joy is done in the small moments, there is still a part of me that won't let go of thinking that the big moments are the most important ones. It's the part of me that believes my overall trend would catapult forward if I could just have that house by the water. It doesn't even have to be a big body of water, or a big house, but I just know I would be happier living by the sea. No, wait—I know. The lottery. If I could just win the lottery, I could have the house by the sea, a cleaning service, no laundry to do . . . and *then* I would be soooooo happy!

Yes, a prime example of big moment thinking: believing the winning lottery ticket would shift the overall trend. The big moments do create a blip in the line and give us a jolt of happiness for a period of time, but they do not tend to last. Studies of people who have won the lottery confirm that their happiness goes up after they win but a year later it returns to the same level it was before they won.[23] I know all these facts but part of me can't bring myself to totally believe it. I think to myself, "Well, maybe that was true for them, but I'm different and my happiness would last." Part of me still wants to win the lottery. Well, let's just say I wouldn't turn the money down. Ingrained cultural beliefs die hard.

We are a destination culture. This observation was made by Lucy Walker, director of the documentary movie *Blindsight*, which is about the ascent of Mount Everest by blind Tibetan climbers and their guides. In an article for the *Toronto Star* she wrote:

> *Westerners can't just succeed anymore. They have to follow every success with another one. Westerners who visit Mt. Everest think of only one thing—reaching the summit no matter the cost. Our obsession with "success" puzzles Tibetans who prefer to walk around mountains.*[24]

Walker explains that Tibetans would not be on top of mountains if it were not for Westerners, who pay the Sherpas large sums of money for their assistance with the climb. In the West, we have bought into the myth that happiness comes when we achieve the big milestones. For example, we decide that we don't make enough money in our current job and if we just had a better job that paid more, then our lives would be happier. Or we feel our body is looking old, overweight, or otherwise displeasing and if we could just get in shape and look younger, then we would be happy. Or if my partner were more ____ (fill in the blank) then I would be happy. So we get books and seek out experts, trying to do and be and have certain things, all in the name of feeling better. Sometimes they help and sometimes they don't. We spend a lot of life trying to figure it all out, and some of us never do.

We go after the big milestones that look like upward blips in the curve, not realizing they don't shift the overall trend. They temporarily make us happier, but they don't have staying power. We end up sacrificing the small moments in between that really matter and help build momentum for change.

An interesting thing happened for several participants as they began to experience more joy. They found themselves in an upward spiral. Joy acted like a catalyst that propelled them forward in other areas of their lives:

> There are a number of side benefits that started because of the study. I began exercising more . . . so I was physically and mentally feeling much better. Also, I began doing more in terms of connecting with some groups in our church.

> I feel more energized to keep looking for the work I want, and at the same time I feel better about the work I am doing.

> Physically I felt much healthier, and found myself snacking on healthier foods, and getting in more exercise (in spite of a hectic schedule), etc.

Good feelings have an upward spiraling effect. As you feel better, you become more motivated and inspired to make positive changes in your life. Bob Greene is a well-known personal trainer whom Oprah Winfrey credits for her weight loss. In his book *The Best Life Diet*, he says:

If you're like most people, you're probably trying to lose weight so that you look better and feel better about yourself— that is, you want to be happy. But weight loss alone cannot make you happy. Sure, losing weight will boost your confidence and self-esteem for a short time, but real joy is only going to come to you if you clear up the issues in your life that send you running to the refrigerator.[25]

He then puts it beautifully: "Losing weight isn't the key to happiness—happiness is the key to losing weight":[26] whether we want to lose weight, get organized, or reinvent ourselves, the best place to begin is by getting happier. Can you see how this works? Don't you feel more motivated to stick with a diet or head to the gym when you're feeling really good about yourself? Isn't it when life goes in the tank that you want to binge or drink or escape in any number of ways? So many times we try to put the cart before the horse and make big changes in order to feel better. A good place to begin is with these exercises to increase happiness, which then help propel us toward whatever other changes we need to make.

Which brings us to the question: How happy can we really get? How far up can the upward trend go? Psychology researchers have developed a concept called the happiness set point.[27] This term describes the average happiness level we are born with, and it acts like a rubber band in that we tend to bounce back to it no matter what happens to us. Researchers hypothesize that this set point accounts for about half of our happiness experience, and that it is fundamentally unchangeable. In other words, if you were born a depressed pessimist, approximately half of your experience will never change.

One equation for estimating the factors that determine happiness suggests that 50 percent is the result of the hereditary factors just described, 10 percent is the result of life circumstances such as marital status, gender, age, health, income, significant life events, and so on, and the final 40 percent is the result of our own intentional activity.[28] In other words, 40 percent of our experience is within our control to change.

While I greatly respect this work and believe it is adding incredible value to the field of psychology, my own work, and the world at large, I have to disagree with the conclusion about the possibilities for change. I believe we can change most, if not all, of our experience. I think the unchangeable part that is due to heredity is helpful from a descriptive perspective, but not a predictive one. In other words, I can agree that a portion of our disposition may very well be genetically determined, but that does not mean we can't change it. It simply describes how we got to where we are, but it does not dictate where we can go.

I make this claim based on two factors. First, my own experience. My average happiness for over three quarters of my life was in the lowest part of any happiness scale you care to pick, and I am now solidly in the upper range. When you do the math, it means I've improved my overall happiness by more than 50 percent.

The second factor is the new research on neuroplasticity. Neurologists used to agree that the brain was relatively fixed and stable, but now they are coming to the conclusion that it is "plastic" and can grow and regenerate in ways never before thought possible.[29] This new research is providing mounting evidence that not only can happiness be learned, but over time the brain can actually be permanently altered to embed the changes.[30] It takes time to make permanent changes, and preliminary research suggests it can take as much as six months of regular practiced activity to form new neuronal connections.[31] Since the idea of intentionally doing "happiness exercises" is such a new concept, it is not surprising that few if any people who have applied this kind of intervention for an extended period of time have ever been studied.

The new brain research suggests we can get at that 50 percent of the set point that is supposedly hardwired. It just takes concerted and repeated effort to form new brain maps. *Newsweek* science writer Sharon Begley agrees in her book *Train Your Mind, Change Your Brain:*

> *If scientists find time and again that people return to their baseline level of happiness, maybe that's because they are studying people who, like virtually every Westerner, have no clue that one can sculpt the brain's emotional circuitry as powerfully as one can sculpt one's pectoral muscles.*[32]

The reason I am going on about this is that I don't want people to limit themselves by thinking that only 40 percent change is possible. As Henry Ford said, "Whether you think you can or you think you can't, either way you're right." If you believe you can only shift 40 percent of your happiness, then you're right. While a 40 percent shift is enough for many people to live a happy and fulfilled life, why settle for less when you don't have to?

I find the neuroplasticity advancements fascinating, and am keeping a close watch on new developments. I believe there is a lot we will soon learn about undoing and recreating new thought patterns, which is at the heart of creating joy. Right now the knowledge is highly anecdotal, and that is why so much of this book contains personal stories rather than research. It will be nice eventually to be able to talk about electrodes and lab rats rather than myself for a change.

As I mentioned before, my personal set point has increased substantially over time. I have been on this journey for a while. When I first began trying to create more joy, progress was painfully slow. I did not have all the tools and insights I have now, and I imagine that was a big part of it. But regardless, the beginning of any major change requires considerable effort in undoing lots of habits and thinking patterns to the contrary. It can be likened to trying to turn a large ocean freighter. That initial push to get it going in a different direction takes the most effort, but once it starts turning it begins to gain momentum.

As I continued on the journey by using a variety of exercises and interventions, I started to feel some momentum building. Then all of a sudden everything started to click and my happiness began to increase exponentially. Let me plot it out for you:

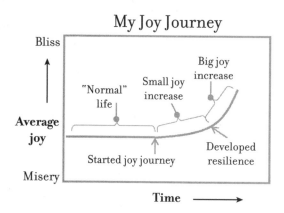

Please note that I'm still working with a sample size of one, but the upward acceleration I experienced at one point in the journey was rather dramatic. When I began inquiring into what happened to spark the upward shift, I came across the work of Barbara Fredrickson at the University of North Carolina in Chapel Hill. She is a top positive psychology researcher who has done significant work on a concept she calls the Broaden and Build theory.[33] Her theory contains a number of fascinating and relevant concepts about happiness, but for the sake of this discussion I want to focus on her notion of resilience. I think my upward spike in happiness occurred when I developed resilience.

Fredrickson studied the happiness level of people before and after the terrorist attacks of September 11, 2001, and found that resilient people came out of that crisis stronger than they went in. "They emerged from their anguish more satisfied with life, more optimistic, and more tranquil—and likely more resilient—than before."[34] She suggests we can build resilience by increasing our positive emotion, and that is exactly what happened to me.

I have been aware of a definite shift in my ratio of positive to negative thoughts over time and I have learned how to frame difficulties in a more appreciative light. This became readily apparent a few months ago when I got a call from my doctor. You always want to get a call from the nurse, not the doctor, because the doctor doesn't usually call unless it's serious. The last time a doctor called was about twenty years ago to tell me I had melanoma.

This time it was to tell me I had an "abnormal" mammogram. They had found a small mass and needed to do an ultrasound to get more information. I was thrown by the call and found myself upset and shaky. I was quite scared and started crying as I went to tell Jon.

I then got out my pen and paper as I do when anything hits me hard, and I started thinking through the situation. I began to challenge my story to try to find some good in it all. Coincidentally, I had just read an article on breast cancer, and one of the things it said was that the success rate for treatment was high if caught early. My doctor had said the mass was small, so I knew if it was anything, it was in the early stages. I came to the conclusion that this was not something I was likely to die from, but it could require a mastectomy with chemo and/or radiation. While this was hardly good news, the realization that I would likely survive brought me some comfort.

Then I began thinking about what might be ahead, and I wondered how I could use my appreciative living exercises through it all. I imagined myself with other women in treatment and support groups and thought about how I could share what I've learned with them. I actually started feeling a bit excited about the possibility of helping others, and began to see how this could be a wonderful application for the work. I could document everything I did and maybe even create a program out of it for other cancer patients. As much as I did not want the experience, I could also see how I could use it in a positive way. This took a great deal of the pain and fear out of my story, and I was able to let go and trust that whatever would be, would be. As it turned out, everything was fine and nothing further needed to be done.

This ability to find the good in bad situations was a real turning point for me. I am at the point where I know in my gut that when anything bad happens, there is an important learning or opportunity contained within. I still get angry and upset when bad things happen, but I can almost always find the silver lining.

I have also come to see that if I am stuck in one place, it

means I am stuck in that area in the rest of my life. For example, if I am struggling with patience in the grocery line, you can bet it is showing up in my parenting, teaching, and every other relationship. Knowing that an issue I face in any particular situation is universal gives me added incentive to work through it, since I know it will raise the bar in all other areas of my life.

I've been at this a while, but I believe we can all learn to find more of the good in bad situations. The negative emotions don't go away, but I find I move through them much faster. I also don't get as upset about as many things as I used to before. I get a tremendous sense of peace and calm from believing at a deep level that I can learn from any situation and it will ultimately make my life better. That belief is central to my ability to see the positive core and inherent possibilities in situations. And it can be yours by doing the exercises regularly.

The Positive Principle suggests that positive emotion is essential for effective change, and the exercises help you build positive emotion by focusing on the positive core. They also accelerate your journey to happiness, since feeling good inspires you to make needed changes in other areas of your life. This is very exciting news, as it speaks to the concept of leverage. Just a few minutes of appreciation, appreciative questions, and visualization can spiral into significant long-term change.

Mahatma Gandhi said, "There is no path to peace. Peace is the path." I like to play off this and say, "There is no path to joy. Joy is the path." It is an ever upward journey and not a destination. If you stay with it, your ability to create joy gains momentum over time, and the sky is the limit.

Doesn't it just make you want to get started right now?

7

Happiness Versus Joy

I wanted to escape from it all . . . maybe go work at a retreat center,
or live on a tropical island. I thought it would be magical. I went
to a spiritual place for a bit, and when I returned I realized that
the magic is here—inside. Are you going to stay in your space of
centeredness and joy or be knocked off? I wanted to escape
from it all, but there is no place to go; it's all right here.
—Study participant

During the study a distinction between happiness and joy emerged. And while I'd like to say it came about from in-depth research or deep reflection, it actually was inspired by a greater source of learning for me than even my bookshelf: my children.

Early on in the study I decided that I would do the exercises with my son and daughter, who were six and eight years old at the time. The first day I began by asking them to list three things they appreciated, and I dutifully wrote down their answers. On my daughter's list was our fish, cleverly named Fishy, the neighbor's dog Chester, and that we were going out to dinner that night. My son appreciated chocolate milk, LEGO Building Blocks, and that he was going to have a great time today. That part went fairly well.

Then I asked the daily question of what one thing they could do to increase their joy. This is where things got interesting.

My daughter said, "Go to the pool and go down the slide," and my son said, "Eat lots of ice cream." They both got really excited as they considered these possibilities, and I got really uncomfortable. I was in charge of the daily activities, and the pool and ice cream were nowhere on the agenda. I wasn't sure what to do about it, so I did nothing.

The next day came and I tried again. The appreciation list went well, and they easily came up with new things like "Mommy vacuumed the house," "I can't wait to have breadsticks for dinner," and "We have light." Then it came time for the question of how to increase joy, and it got dicey again. My daughter said, "Go roller skating and not wear any pads," and my son reiterated, "Eats lots of ice cream." I could see the excitement in their eyes as they came up with these great ideas, and I began to squirm. Roller skating and ice cream were not going to happen, but I started to wonder if maybe I should try to make them happen so the kids would not be disappointed. Once again, I did nothing.

Day three. The appreciation list came easily, and to increase joy it was lots of cookies and lots of ice cream. I wondered if they were ever going to catch on to the fact that what they wanted never happened, but it didn't seem like it. They seemed as happy as ever as they considered the possibility of eating cookies and ice cream all day. Once again, I did not attempt to make their dreams come true.

Day four. Same thing. Easy appreciation list, cookies and ice cream. I couldn't take it anymore. I felt like the worst mother in the world. Here I was asking my children to figure out what would bring them joy, and then when they came up with something I never let it happen. I decided to quit asking them the questions. Had I known then what I know now, I would have continued the exercises. But instead I panicked.

All of a sudden it hit me that I had lots of people across the country doing these exercises, too. What if they were having the same disappointing experience? I ran into the den and scrambled to try to make sense of what was going on.

If I've learned nothing else from my children, I've learned they are like mini versions of adults in many ways. Robert Fulghum's book *All I Really Need to Know I Learned in Kindergarten* says it all. So I asked myself: How is it that I ask for the proverbial ice cream every day?

The answer began to emerge. I came to see that anytime I ask for something that is essentially outside of my control, it is like them asking for ice cream. It happens any time I put my hope of happiness in the hands of someone or something else. I started making a list of examples, and let me tell you, there were a lot of them. Like "If I can just avoid traffic delays I'll enjoy my commute today." Or "If there's no line at the coffee shop I would love to grab a cup on my way." Or "If I can get all the things done on my to-do list I'll feel so much better." Or my personal favorite: "If I could just have a house on the water I would be so happy." When we hang our hopes for happiness on things that are outside of our control, we set ourselves up for disappointment. It's not that the ice cream or the lake house won't make us happy for a short period of time; it's that these things are essentially outside of our control. When we need the ice cream to be happy, we put our happiness at the mercy of whoever is in charge of the freezer. We give up our power. We let go of our responsibility for joy. This is a very vulnerable place to be, and we end up becoming dependent on others for our happiness. And let me tell you, it happens a lot more often than you might think. At least that was my experience.

Despite their not getting their ice cream or cookies, I have to say that over the four days I did the exercises with my children, they never once seemed the least bit disappointed. So there is another piece to this. The first part is thinking happiness comes from getting what we want; the second part is attaching to it. In other words, if I get the ice cream I will be happy, but if I don't, then it's sour grapes. The more attached we are to an outcome, the more dependent we become on it, and the bigger the disappointment when it doesn't happen. As English engraver, illustrator, and poet William Blake said:

> *He who binds to himself a joy,*
> *does the winged life destroy.*
> *But he who kisses the joy as it flies,*
> *lives in eternity's sun rise.*

It was interesting to me that my children did not attach to the outcome, at least within the four-day period. They continued to be just as happy and excited to answer the question the next day even though they never once got what they had asked for.

This prompted further reflection on my part. I now understood the attachment piece, but what exactly was happiness? I started feeling like the Grinch, who at first thinks Christmas is about presents and food, but later comes to learn that it is something much more. I knew that happiness was much more than cookies, beach houses, and huge bank accounts, but what exactly was it? What was I trying to help all these people find?

Before you think I am about to reveal the secret to happiness, let me manage your expectations up front. Philosophers, theologians, and psychologists have been debating this for centuries. It is like the story of the blind men and the elephant, where five blind men all grab a different part of an elephant, and then describe what they have. One takes hold of a leg and says it is a pillar, another holds the tail and thinks it is a rope, and so on.

Each person who gives a definition of the "joy elephant" is coming at it from a different perspective, story, and set of beliefs. So there is no one right answer. On top of that, it is an experience we are trying to describe, and definitions only go so far in describing experience. Having said all this, it is very helpful, in fact it is essential, to embark on the journey of defining it for ourselves. The insights others have about joy can help us come up with a definition that fits who we are. Let's take a brief look at what a few experts have to say on the matter.

In his book *Authentic Happiness*, Martin Seligman suggests there are two distinct types of happiness. The first is what he calls the pleasures,[35] which is what I would call the ice cream. They are the external things that are outside of our control, like great jobs and lake houses and massages and vacations and having our spouse remember our birthday. They create temporary happiness, and to the extent we are attached to them, a dependent kind of happiness. They can add to our sense of pleasure when we get them, but the feeling doesn't last.

The second type of happiness he calls the gratifications.[36] According to his definition, we experience this type of happiness when we are totally absorbed in what we are doing. It might be getting immersed in a good book, experiencing a breathtaking sunset, or doing a challenging rock climb. We lose ourselves in the moment, and there isn't necessarily an emotion associated with the experience. In fact, many people describe it as a sense of being out of touch with time, and some describe it as a spiritual experience. Psychology professor and researcher Mihály Csíkszentmihályi describes it as being in a state of flow.[37] The gratifications were getting closer to the kind of happiness I was trying to name, but I still felt there was something more to be said about it.

Tal Ben-Shahar, author of *Happier: Learn the Secrets to Daily Joy and Lasting Fulfillment,* is another respected expert in the field of happiness and a popular lecturer at Harvard University. He says:

> I define happiness as "the overall experience of pleasure and meaning." A happy person enjoys positive emotions while perceiving her life as purposeful. The definition does not pertain to a single moment but to a generalized aggregate of one's experiences: a person can endure emotional pain at times and still be happy overall.[38]

Ben-Shahar combines the pleasures and gratifications with an additional emphasis on moving toward a meaningful destination. He says, "Attaining lasting happiness requires that we enjoy the *journey* on our way toward a *destination* we deem valuable."[39] I like the addition of the journey, as it includes enjoyment of the small moments which I've discussed in previous chapters. But still I felt there was something more.

I began reading through the joy study results to see what participants had to say. As I read the quotes from participants on what brought them joy, I began to feel my heart swell. Most of them had been out of touch with what really made them happy, and the joy exercises had initiated a journey of discovery as they began to connect to a deeper inner knowing. The quotes seemed to speak to a universal journey, and yet the way it showed up in people's lives was as varied as they were. Joy was found in many places, and here is what people had to say.

Joy is . . .

- *Being centered and feeling whole as I go about my day.*
- *A peaceful existence.*
- *Something that makes my heart lighter or makes me smile to myself.*
- *A commitment to smile, a love of life no matter what.*
- *Total happiness and peace. Fulfillment.*
- *Things that give me a sense of peace and delight.*
- *A glimpse of happiness, if only for a short period of time. A powerful, peaceful feeling within the very core of my soul that makes everything feel right . . . like I'm on the right path.*
- *Having a sense of wonder in the world, feeling humbled and confident/proud at the same time, carrying a bold sense of purpose and commitment to the world.*

People described a feeling that was more about being than doing, a combination of peace, happiness, and wholeness with a deep, centered quality. It had a sense of power, but with a feeling of contentment and fulfillment at the same time. As I read through the quotes I could see it had a place of its own, but I wasn't sure how to distinguish it from happiness. Seligman's gratitudes didn't capture the depth, and happiness was clearly too highly associated with the external, temporary experiences.

You probably have heard how Eskimos have lots of words to distinguish the different types of snow, and that Native Americans have many words to distinguish the various kinds of rain and wind. Unfortunately, we don't have many distinct words in the English language for joy, so the possibilities are limited.

I went back to my bookshelf to look further. I pulled out

Rachel Remen's *Kitchen Table Wisdom*, a beautiful book about her work with cancer patients and the amazing insights she had in working with them. One passage in particular caught my eye:

> *I am surprised to have found a sort of willingness to show up for whatever life may offer and meet with it rather than wishing to edit and change the inevitable . . . When people begin to take such an attitude they seem to become intensely alive, intensely present . . . From such people I have learned a new definition of the word "joy." I had thought joy to be rather synonymous with happiness, but it seems now to be far less vulnerable than happiness. Joy seems to be a part of an unconditional wish to live, not holding back because life may not meet our preferences and expectations. Joy seems to be a function of the willingness to accept the whole, and to show up to meet with whatever is there . . . It is the lover drunk with the opportunity to love despite the possibility of loss, the player for whom playing has become more important than winning or losing . . . Joy seems more closely related to aliveness than to happiness.*[40]

That was it. I found my word and the word was *joy*. It more fully captures the depth of the participants' experience than what we typically attribute to the word *happiness*. As I mentioned in the introduction, I interchange happiness and joy throughout the book for variety, even though I see them as distinct. I struggled quite a bit with this decision, because it seems like I'm reinforcing the overlap of the very words I'm trying to distinguish. But in the end ease of reading won out over exact terminology, even in the title.

Another thing I love in Rachel Remen's passage above is the notion of aliveness rather than happiness as a synonym for joy.

There was one person in the study who picked up on the connection between aliveness and joy:

> *Being alive is great—to me that's not just happiness, that is joy. Ask yourself, "What could I do today to be more alive? Really alive?" People don't picture themselves in the business of being alive . . . It's not something a lot of people consider or even think about. People talk about going through their lives, but they're not conscious. They don't recognize the experience they are getting, but more importantly, giving. It's always better to give than receive. I'm giving experiences as well as getting them. The question is "What are you giving?"*

He also adds an interesting twist by looking at how we give—I can't think of a better thing to give than a joyful outlook. Ralph Waldo Emerson said, "What you are stands over you the while, and thunders so that I cannot hear what you say to the contrary." While we can't control others, the greatest influence we have is who we are in their presence. As Emerson suggests, people learn from what we do and not what we say. We are always giving ourselves to others, whether we are aware of it or not. If we are being joy, we are giving it.

When we detach from outcomes and look for the beauty in simple moments, we find a deeper, more permanent source of internal joy that is distinct from external happiness. As we step into this place we become more alive, and we light the way for others to do the same. Is there a more valuable undertaking in all the world? I wonder if that's what Thomas Aquinas was thinking when he said, "Joy is the human's noblest act." Really, now, can you think of anything more important?

Part Two

WHAT YOU NEED TO

{ Do }

8

Exercise 1: The Daily Appreciation List

I felt that by starting each day with gratitude exercises, I was anticipating joy more intentionally. The daily pause helped frame the day to encounter more joy.
—*Study participant*

And now the moment you've been waiting for: The exercises! In the next five chapters I am going to give you everything you need to get started. chapters 8 through 10 provide a detailed overview of each exercise, including where it came from, why it works, and ways you can modify it to keep it interesting. In chapter 11, I provide seven different tips for helping you stay on track, because let's face it: The hardest part is not the exercises themselves; it's getting yourself to do them! Finally, in chapter 12 I show you how to incorporate the exercises into your daily life after the twenty-eight days so you can continue to create even greater joy.

Before you embark on any of the exercises, you may want to take a baseline happiness test to assess your starting point. While no assessment can accurately quantify happiness, if you take the test repeatedly over time it can provide a relative measure of progress. New and better assessments are constantly being developed; the one I like to use currently is the Oxford Happiness Questionnaire. You'll find a copy of it in Appendix E: Oxford Happiness Questionnaire, with information on how to self-score. You can also take it at www.AppreciativeLiving.com.

In this chapter we'll explore the first exercise, the Appreciation List, whose purpose is to shift your thinking toward what's right with your world rather than what's wrong, similar to a gratitude list. The power of this exercise comes from the heart, as you make an effort to feel grateful for the things on your list. The exercise follows, and is also included as an easy reference in Appendix B. You can also sign up for a free twenty-eight-day program at www.AppreciativeLiving.com where you will receive daily e-mails to help you complete your exercises and assessments.

The Daily Appreciation List:

Each morning, take a minute to get comfortable and relaxed. Get out your preferred means of documentation, whether it's a pen and paper, journal, or computer. Write the date at the top, and list three things you are grateful for. Then take thirty seconds to close your eyes and really focus on and feel your appreciation for each one.

You need to think of three new items or people for your list every day in order to build your "appreciative muscle." It is best to write your answers down, as doing so reinforces them. A written list also provides a nice reference for tracking your progress over time, and becomes a resource of positive inspiration you can review in a low moment to help you feel better.

I had study participants do the exercises in the morning, which helped them start off on the right foot and set up a positive momentum that carried into the rest of the day:

> *I (re)learned that starting my morning off on a positive note is very conducive to having a good day overall. I had known that before, but it must have become unimportant and gotten lost along the way.*

> *I think you can't help but start the day on a positive note when you do the two small exercises religiously.*

If you are more of a night person you can do them in the evening, the advantage being that you go into your sleep relaxed and joyful, and the ideas can simmer in your subconscious while you sleep. But I urge you to try it in the morning for the first two weeks so you can see what works best for you. If you are new to this, or are in a difficult place in your life, it can be hard to come up with things to be grateful for. There is a definite learning curve, and finding the good will get easier over time, as one participant shares:

> *The experience of waking each day with the task of describing three things I was thankful for was, at first, quite unnatural. However, I found that the more I did the exercises, the more I'd look forward to doing them again . . . Thinking positively and concentrating on what I'm thankful for puts many of the*

day's challenges into perspective. In a word, I'd describe the
experience as transforming.

Finding the experience transforming—that would be one good reason to do it. As I've discussed before, we have habitual ways of seeing the world, and we are culturally conditioned to pay attention to what's wrong and broken. It takes regular practice to shift this perspective and begin noticing what's right, and doing this simple exercise is an incredibly powerful way to make that happen.

My neighbor recently used a version of the appreciation exercise to help her nine-year-old daughter, Beckett. Beckett played soccer, and although she enjoyed herself at the games, she would complain about having to practice. After a few weeks my neighbor had finally heard enough whining and decided to try an appreciative approach. She told her daughter that she was now well-versed on all her gripes and complaints, and from now on they were going to try something different. Beckett had to come up with at least one thing she liked prior to each practice session. It could be anything, even if it was just that her shorts were comfortable.

It was a slow go at first, as Beckett reluctantly complied through clenched teeth with things like "I guess the weather is okay." My neighbor did her best to build on whatever her daughter offered up, adding things like, "Yes, it is a beautiful day to be outside running around with your friends in the fresh air."

Beckett started to warm up to the idea after a few weeks, and she began coming up with a number of positive things to say about soccer. The complaining had ended, and best of all, she started to enjoy herself a lot more. It is a great illustration of how

a simple shift in focus to the positive, however small and reluc-
tant it might be, can spiral into a good experience.

Finding the good in a situation is the key to reframing the
situation appreciatively. If you really want to change your way of
thinking, it is important that you give your full attention to the
exercise. Feel your gratitude deeply after thoughtfully making
your list. Focused attention is required in order to create permanent changes in your brain thought patterns, as Norman
Doidge explains in *The Brain That Changes Itself*:

> *In numerous experiments he [neuroplastician Michael
> Merzenich] found that lasting changes occurred only when his
> monkeys paid close attention. When the animals performed
> tasks automatically, without paying attention, they changed
> their brain maps, but the changes did not last. We often praise
> "the ability to multitask." While you can learn when you divide
> your attention, divided attention doesn't lead to abiding change
> in your brain maps.*[41]

Giving your undivided attention is important in making the
changes stick. We're only talking five minutes total for the two
morning exercises, so if you want them to have lasting impact
you need to dedicate yourself to the activity fully. Having said
that, you can still experience short-term benefit by doing it
half-focused, which is better than not doing it all.

If you want to shorten the exercises, you are better off listing just one thing you appreciate and really feeling the emotion
around it than casually listing three things and feeling nothing more than that you're checking one more item off your to-do
list. It's more about quality than quantity.

After you do the appreciation exercise for a period of time, you may find yourself losing interest. I talk more about this in chapter 11, and provide tips for staying on track. Novelty is important, but I would suggest you do the exercise as originally written for at least twenty-eight days, or, ideally, several months, before trying the variations. When you feel steeped in the appreciation experience and are ready for a change, you can try the following two variations.

Appreciation List Variation #1:

Rather than listing three items, write a whole rambling page on someone in your life and what you appreciate about that person. When you are done, consider giving it to him or her. I can't think of a better birthday present.

Appreciation List Variation #2:

Pick a relatively short word for the day that suggests something you appreciate, such as joy, rain, cat, phone, and so on, and make an acrostic gratitude list. You simply write the letters vertically and then list one thing you are grateful for that begins with the letter. It looks like this:

J—Jon (my husband)
O—Oreo cookies
Y—Yellow sunshine

After you list the items, close your eyes and take thirty seconds to feel your appreciation for each one. Remember that whatever you focus on grows, so I would not list something like Oreo cookies unless I wanted that to be part of my experience shortly!

You'll find free templates for these exercise variations on my website www.AppreciativeLiving.com, and a summary of all the exercises is provided for quick reference in Appendix B. Again, I suggest you do the exercises as originally written for at least twenty-eight days, and then play around with them in whatever way works for you.

Working with the Appreciation List is one of the most powerful ways of sifting through our mountain of reality to find the gems. What a precious gift we have in the blank slate of the present moment. It lies waiting for us to write in what we will. What will you draft next? I suggest you begin with an Appreciation List to mine the moment and go digging for gold.

9

Exercise 2: The Daily Question

*I was able to laugh at something my kids did that otherwise
would have made me very frustrated and angry. My "one thing"
for increasing joy that day was to "take my children as they
are and enjoy them." So I thought of that goal when this thing
happened and was able to reach for the parent I strive to
be all the time instead of the reactive parent I am
when I feel most unhappy about life.*
—Study participant

The second exercise in the study is the daily question, and
its purpose is to begin living into joy. The question helps us set
an intention to create happiness for that day and then see what
works to make it happen. It is a simple practice and helps make
the necessary changes in our thoughts and actions to create our
ideal vision. I would suggest you do this exercise immediately
following the Appreciation List, so that you go into the question
with a positive disposition. The exercise follows, and can also be
easily referred to in Apprendix B: Exercise Summary.

The Daily Question Exercise:

Each morning, take a minute to get comfortable and relax.
Get out your preferred means of expression, whether it's a pen
and paper, journal, or computer. Write the date at the top, and
then take two to three minutes to reflect on your answer to the
following question and write it down: "What one thing could I
do today, no matter how small, that would increase my joy?"

Take a few minutes to think about your answer to this question and then write it down. People often ask me, "Do I actually have to do what I write down?" The answer is, "That's up to you." Following through on what you wrote will accelerate your progress, but don't beat yourself up if you continue to miss the mark. There is a lot you can learn by observing what it is that keeps you from doing your one thing. Here is what happened for one participant:

At first, I would list things to do to bring joy, but I wouldn't
get around to them, so I would put them on the next day's list,
but didn't do it then either. That would go on for a while, so that
by the time I actually did them, they seemed more like a burden
or responsibility and not so much like joy. So I switched to ways
to make the things I already had planned for the day more joyful
(which was mostly just an attitude thing) and that seemed to
work better for me.

The most important thing is that you keep answering the question each day. Stay with it, whether you do what you write or not.

Over time your thinking and awareness will begin to shift in valuable ways. And action follows thought.

The daily question also does two important things in the quest for greater happiness. First, it takes you out of autopilot so you can check in with your life and pay attention to what is really going on. It gives you a moment to pause and reflect on your day ahead and look at it through the lens of joy. The second thing the question does is help you get clear about what really does and does not bring joy. As I mentioned earlier, we have many cultural myths that point us in the wrong direction of finding happiness. By asking yourself the question each day, and then testing out what you think will bring you happiness, you find what really works and what doesn't. In the end, the only way of finding your real joy is testing it out.

You may also discover that you sort of fake yourself out sometimes. In *Stumbling on Happiness*, Harvard psychologist Daniel Gilbert summarizes the research on perceived happiness. One of his many findings is that we tend to think we will be happier during the good times than we actually are, and we tend to think the bad times will be worse than they actually turn out to be. He says:

> *We overestimate how happy we will be on our birthdays, we underestimate how happy we will be on Monday mornings, and we make these mundane but erroneous predictions again and again, despite their regular disconfirmation.*[42]

After reading this, I did my own little inquiry and discovered I am guilty of this way of thinking. I decided to test this out one dreary Monday morning when I got out of bed to face the week ahead. My spirits were a bit down as I realized the weekend was over and I was more behind in just about everything than I cared to admit. I brushed my teeth and thought about the research Gilbert cited, and made a mental note to be cognizant of my actual experience throughout the morning. What I found surprised me.

My morning wasn't really all that bad once I got into it. I found myself working steadily through my tasks and I had some feelings of accomplishment after completing a few of them. There were several moments when I felt down or frustrated, but they didn't last long once I immersed myself in activity. While the morning was not nirvana, it was not quite the drudgery I had imagined. I had pictured the bad stuff to be worse than it actually turned out to be.

I then decided to try it on the other end. We had a beach vacation coming up that I was really, really looking forward to, and I spent time dreaming and intentionally visualizing how it was going to be—so wonderful and relaxing. When the time came, I decided I would mentally check in throughout the vacation to see how happy I really was. Again, I was a bit surprised.

I would classify the vacation as one of my best ever, but there definitely were moments that were less than perfect. I even remember being bored a few times, and there were a few experiences that were downright stressful. I wrote about the experience in a series called "Appreciative Living: Getting Started," available at no cost at www.AppreciativeLiving.com. I could see how I sort of glossed over the unpleasant moments that came up, but I wasn't so much disappointed by this as I was intrigued. It was a great vacation, but it wasn't as perfect as the vacation I had imagined.

My point is not that we need to have more realistic expectations about good or bad future events, but to point out how out of
touch we are in general to our honest happiness level. If we simply check in to see how we are *actually* feeling throughout the
day, and not how we *think* we are feeling, we can learn a lot about
what really brings joy and what doesn't. All the information we
need is right in front of us: We just need to pay attention. And
the daily question helps us do that.

As simple as this little insight may sound, it has helped me
raise my happiness in some of the small moments. Anytime I
have a dentist appointment or something less than desirable
coming up, I make a mental note to remember that it probably
will not be as bad as I imagine. I find this brings a bit of relief
when I'm feeling anxious.

On the other end, I also let go of having perfect peak experiences. When the big vacation or holidays or other highly anticipated events come, I now know there will likely be moments that
are less than what I imagined in my perfect scenario, and that
is okay. It helps me to accept whatever shows up without feeling the need to resist it in order to preserve the "ideal bubble" I
seem to hold on to at some level. That reminds me of one of my
favorite movies.

I love the movie *National Lampoon's Christmas Vacation* because I identify with it so closely. It is the story of a man named
Clark Griswold, played by Chevy Chase, who is determined
to create the perfect family Christmas. He goes to ridiculous
extremes to make it happen, and as one thing after another falls
apart, you watch him desperately trying to make it work. The
holiday gathering finally gets so bad, he loses his temper and the
whole charade comes tumbling down. Amid the rubble, he has

a touching conversation with his dad, where they both admit that all their holidays were a mess. This heartfelt moment is more real than the facade he has tried so hard to maintain. It is also the point at which he can finally begin to enjoy the holiday for what it truly is and not what he wishes it were. It is a great exaggeration of how we attach perfect images to our not-so-perfect lives, and then get disappointed when something else happens.

An important first step in the joy journey is learning to accept whatever shows up, which does not mean agreeing with, rolling over for, or otherwise giving power to what is happening. It does mean seeing simply what is there without all of the negative judgments about whether it should be happening or not. It's noticing what's going on without fighting against it, wishing it weren't happening, ignoring it altogether, or any one of the many things we do to resist or deny reality.

It's essentially saying something like, "Oh—look what showed up. What can I appreciate about this?" I'm being somewhat cavalier and oversimplifying this tremendously. But if you can grasp the idea that it is more effective to work with whatever happens rather than fight against it, you can begin to soften your adverse reactions to negative situations and become open to new possibilities. We know from the Poetic Principle that the good stuff is in there somewhere, but we have to choose to find it.

The daily question can raise our awareness of what goes on in our lives and the extent to which we are really happy or not. You'll find you can continue to ask this question for quite some time before you tire of it. As with all the exercises, however, there may come a point where you want a little variety. In that case, you can shift the question as follows:

Daily Question Variation #1

Vary the daily question as follows: "What one thing can I do, no matter how small, to move me in the direction of ____?" (Fill in the blank with whatever you want more of in your life, such as better health, greater abundance, more loving relationships, and so on.)

Daily Question Variation #2

Vary the daily question as follows: "What one thing can I do today, no matter how small, to shift my attention to ____?" (Fill in the blank with whatever you want more of in your life, such as better health, greater abundance, more loving relationships, and so on.)

I suggest you ask the daily question as originally written for an extended period of time before varying it. As mentioned in previous chapters, getting happier is the key to making any other changes you desire, so I would spend a good amount of time asking the original question, until you experience a noticeable shift in joy. From your relatively happier place, you are then better equipped and inspired to make other changes in your life.

Finally, I would suggest you take time each week to reflect on your experience with a quick five-minute assessment. You can do this in lieu of the two daily exercises, so it does not add any time to your program. These assessment questions follow, and are also provided in Appendix B for quick reference.

Weekly Assessment:

1. *What two things did you learn from doing the exercises this week?*
2. *How was your week better because you did them?*

When people are asked about their biggest regrets at the end of their lives, it's not about the mistakes and failures they made. It's about the things they did not do, such as missed business opportunities and not spending enough time with friends and family.[43] The daily question will help you figure out what is most meaningful to you in your life, and help you begin taking action to make it happen. Doing the exercises will minimize the chance you will feel regretful over things you wish you had done. One of the few regrets you might have at that point is that you didn't get started sooner.

10

Exercise 3: Weekly Visioning

*The weekly vision exercise is quite powerful and
uplifting. God only knows what would happen if
you continued to do it each week!*
—Study participant

The final exercise in the group is the weekly visioning session. The purpose of this exercise is to get clear about what joy looks like for you, and to create ideal mental pictures in your mind that act as beacons you can gravitate toward. It also gives you some insight into answering the daily question.

Many of you may have done some version of a visioning exercise at one point or another and will find this one pretty straightforward. The key to success with this exercise is making your vision as real as possible, as if it were actually happening.

The Weekly Visioning Exercise:

Once a week, take fifteen to twenty minutes and do the fol-
lowing: Get out your preferred means of documentation, whether
it's a pen and paper, journal, or computer. Begin by getting
yourself comfortable and feeling as good as you can. You might
want to put on some inspiring music, look at pictures that make
you feel happy, or play with your pets. Or you can do the daily
exercises to help you move into a place where you're feeling good.

Now, write the date at the top of your paper, along with this
statement: "This is my ideal, joy-filled life." Pretend that a mir-
acle occurred and your perfect, ideal, joy-filled life manifested
right now before your eyes. Write down every glorious piece you
can imagine about what this ideal life looks like at the highest
level. You only have fifteen minutes, so you have to keep the
vision big. How is your health? Your career? Your relationships?
Your home? List the ideas as they stream through your mind. Let
your deepest hopes and desires come forth and dream big about
your perfect, happy life. Pretend it is really happening now, and
feel the joy inside of you as you write.

Here is one example:

I love my life. I get up each morning, feeling well-rested,
energized, and excited to start the day. I can hardly wait to
begin my work, where I feel so fulfilled and inspired that it
doesn't even feel right to call it work. It is more like a calling—a
passion. I feel like I am changing the world in a meaningful
and wonderful way. And my relationships are extraordinary. I

have so many friends and family members that I love; it is a joy to be alive. My children are so beautiful—like small miracles. We are incredibly close and I thoroughly enjoy the time we spend together. I learn so much from them and enjoy them more the older they get. My husband and I are closer than ever, and when I think our relationship can't get any better, it does. I just love the feeling we have created in our home as well. It is so peaceful and serene, like an oasis from the busyness of life. My physical and mental health is extraordinary, too. I enjoy the activities I do to keep myself in shape and feel much younger than my age would suggest. I've really come to love and accept my body in the aging process and enjoy the advantages of growing older. We regularly take amazing vacations that are fun and rejuvenating, and I think the part that I just can't get over is how fun my life is! I laugh constantly, and find humor in everything. I am so grateful to be alive and living a life beyond my wildest dreams.

This exercise has helped many people get clear about what they really want in their lives; there are more examples of vision statements at www.AppreciativeLiving.com. As I mentioned in the Anticipatory Principle, our images of the future affect the future we experience. If we don't intentionally think about what we want going forward, then the influences of our culture, families, and institutions will complete the picture for us. Doing this exercise puts us in the driver's seat of our lives and helps us become more deliberate about what we are creating. For several in the study, it was an inspirational wake-up call:

Doing the exercises, particularly the visioning, has really helped me to clarify what I want in my life.

*I think that doing this exercise has changed the way I look
at the future. I am genuinely envisioning paths that include
concrete ways to pursue more joyful living.*

*I really enjoyed the once a week life vision. I would really get
engaged in how I envision my future. I always felt better after
completing that exercise.*

Once people got clear about what they wanted, they could begin
visualizing it more effectively. Earlier I discussed how imagining what we want is an effective way to make it happen. In *Get
Out of Your Own Way*, leadership adviser Robert Cooper explains
how visualizing a goal will fire the same neurons in the brain as
the ones we actually need to achieve that goal.[44] He says that one
of the keys to success in this process is emotion.[45] It is essential that we experience authentic good feelings as we create our
ideal mental picture to increase the likelihood of it becoming a
reality. The more real you can make the vision feel, the greater
the chance it will come to pass.

When I talk about the importance of "getting into" your
vision, one question that often surfaces has to do with the idea
of expectations. People want to know at what point a vision
becomes an expectation, and what the difference is between the
two. Let me see if I can shed some light on this. A while back I
was cleaning out some old boxes, and I came across a small puz-
zle I used to love as a child. It had an adorable little puppy on
it, with my all-time favorite quote back then: "Blessed are those
who expect nothing, for they shall not be disappointed." Here
are two of the many ways we can think about this concept.

The first perspective is to ask for nothing and that's just

what you get. Zippo. No disappointment there. No joy, either. It reminds me of the lines from the Simon and Garfunkel song "I Am a Rock": "I am a rock. I am an island. And a rock feels no pain. And an island never cries." You get the picture.

Now the second perspective. Let me substitute the words *attach to* for the word *expect*. Blessed are those who *attach to* nothing, for they shall not be disappointed. Can you see how this might work? It says nothing about dreaming or risking, by the way. The place where a vision often becomes an expectation is when there is an attachment. It's when we decide we have to have this magnificent thing happen or we will not be happy. The point is not to stop wishing and dreaming. The point is to visualize with all your heart, but to detach from the outcome. Easier said than done.

It takes some practice to learn to let go of our visions. It requires that we live into our visualizations completely with every ounce of passion we have, while letting go of the outcome. We have to believe in them with all our heart and soul and yet be okay whether they happen or not. It's a tall order, and in the beginning many of us will find ourselves attaching to our visions in some form or other. But detachment can be learned with deliberate effort.

Then the question becomes: Should we still visualize if we can't detach? In other words, should we go through the process of imagining this wonderful future even though we may be setting ourselves up for disappointment? Let me make the question more obvious. Should we dream small until we get it right? Well, what kind of life is that? It's a small life. Is there a chance you could imagine something you really want and get all tangled up in it and become really disappointed if it doesn't happen exactly the way you thought? Of course. Does that mean you shouldn't dream big? Not in my book. But you have your own story to write.

Over time, the more I visualized, the easier it became to detach. For one, I got better with practice, and I am now at the point where at least part of my vision will typically come to light. I still have stuck points in my belief system, but nothing compared to when I first began. My successful experiences allow me to trust the process to a much greater extent, and that gives me patience to let go and stay the course.

What also happened is that my life started getting a whole lot better from the exercises. The happier I became in the present, the less desperate I was for change in the future. It's ironic, as so many things in life are, but the better I get with visioning, the less I seem to need it. I'm happier in my life right now than I ever dreamed possible, and if I never get any happier it will be just fine. At the same time, I still enjoy imagining a future that is even better than the one I'm living, and while it would be great if it happens, it's also fine if it doesn't. This is letting go of the outcome, and it's definitely easier when things are going well in the present.

There is also an art to visioning, and you will find your groove with practice. There is a fine line between creating an image that is broad enough to allow multiple ways for it to manifest, yet detailed enough to be inspiring and meaningful. An extreme example of an image that is too broad might be something like "I want a joyful life." While this sounds good as a concept, it is not inspiring in and of itself. An image that is too detailed might be "I want a joyful life where I get home at 4:48 on weekdays and dinner is waiting on the table made by a professional chef who lives within four miles of my home and brings fresh organic vegetables every day..." As Goldilocks knows, somewhere in the middle is just right, and you have to find that place for yourself. The example I provided earlier is what I consider to be middle ground; there are several other examples you can read at www.AppreciativeLiving.com.

If you have not done much deliberate visualization before, be patient at the start. Some people find it easier to visualize than others and can quickly create images upon suggestion. For people like this, the difficulty often lies in getting clear about what you want. You can achieve this by continuing to spend time visualizing, and allowing what you want to emerge and become clearer over time.

There are some people who are much less visual in nature, and visualization can be difficult for them. The important point to remember is that emotion is a key part of this exercise. If you can't completely see the image in your mind, but you can really feel or experience the image as if it were happening, the "visualization" will still work. But the imaging skill can be developed with practice.

We now know that the brain is like a muscle, and we can strengthen it with stimulation.[46] Doing visualization exercises can help stimulate and develop the part of our brain responsible for visual imaging, making it easier over time for us to engage naturally in this activity.

For those of you who are struggling to "see" images in your mind, you may want to begin by doing one or both of the bridging exercises that follow. They will build your "visual imaging muscle" and can be used in place of the third visualization exercise if you are having trouble with it.

Visioning Bridge Exercise #1:

Write the following headings on a piece of paper, leaving space between them:

- *Vacations you'd like to take*
- *People you'd like to meet*
- *Food you'd like to try*
- *Places you'd like to go*
- *Relationships you'd like to have*
- *Hobbies you'd like to try*
- *Traits you'd like to develop (patience, love, etc.)*
- *Things you'd like to own*
- *Experiences you'd like to have*
- *Things you'd like to do with your children/spouse/friends/parents/relatives*
- *Add a few of your own categories*

Take fifteen minutes every week to sit down and thoughtfully add items under the headings. After you have added a few items, select one to work with. Close your eyes, and do your best to imagine yourself in this experience. Try to be as detailed as possible, picturing what you might be seeing, doing, saying, smelling, or feeling in the moment.

Visioning Bridge Exercise #2:

Think of someone who has a life you really admire and would love to live. He or she could be famous or not. Reflect on this person's life, and take fifteen minutes to make a list of all the good things you imagine this person must be living. It is not important whether the items on your list are true or not. For example, if you pick Oprah Winfrey, you may list things like "Her work is fascinating, she meets all kinds of interesting people, she lives in the most beautiful homes, she has seemingly thousands of friends, she has people who cook and clean for her and take care of her every need, and she takes amazing vacations."

The following week, go back to the list you made and spend fifteen minutes on the next activity. Pick two things you wrote on the list, and imagine what it would be like if you actually had those things happen in your life. For example, you might select the fact that she meets with all kinds of interesting people, and take a few minutes to close your eyes and imagine what that might be like. Imagine yourself going up to a famous person you admire and having a conversation, or interviewing someone you've always wanted to meet. Really try to put yourself in the situation and feel the excitement of what that would be like. Make it as real as possible.

Continue doing this exercise each week for fifteen minute intervals; it will get easier over time. You will be exercising your imagination, which gets you thinking outside the box to explore possible futures.

After doing one or both of these bridging exercises for a few weeks, try the original exercise again, and keep working at it until you can really feel the emotion around the pictures you've created in your mind.

In the previous chapter I mentioned the importance of

reflecting on your progress each week in order to get the most out of the exercises; I would also suggest you do a more thorough reflection once a month. You can do the assessment below once a month in place of that week's visioning exercise. The assessment consists of a series of questions you can ask yourself to evaluate how your program is going, and whether it would be beneficial to make any changes for the next month. This assessment is also included in Appendix B for easy reference.

Monthly Assessment:

1. *What is working really well in your exercise routine that you'd like to build upon or continue?*

2. *What changes could you make, no matter how small, that would make your experience more effective, interesting, or enjoyable?*

3. *Answer one of the following questions:*
   - *What three to five things are currently bringing you the most joy?*
   - *What are you wondering or curious about at this stage of your journey?*
   - *How is your life getting better?*
   - *What has surprised you in doing the exercises?*
   - *Think of a situation you handled particularly well. What did you do that made it a success and what can you apply from this going forward?*
   - *As you reflect on your overall life vision, pick one part in particular that you are excited about. What is one thing you can do next month to move you forward in this area?*

Doing this assessment will not only enhance the effectiveness of your program; it will also help keep you motivated to continue. If you do it in place of one visioning session it won't add any time, and I strongly suggest you make it a priority.

Once you have mastered the visioning exercise, or, frankly, you're bored with it, you may want to spice it up a bit. As I mentioned in the previous chapters, novelty is important for keeping up with any exercise program. Here are two variations on the visioning exercise you can try:

Visioning Exercise Variation #1:

Perform the original visualization exercise once a month to keep your big picture going, but do mini five-minute visualizations twice a week as follows: Close your eyes and get comfortable, and think about your day ahead. Imagine it unfolding joyfully. See yourself going through the motions of each of your activities in a happy, peaceful manner. Notice how easily you flow from one thing to the next, and see yourself engaging with others in a kind and loving way. Observe everything getting done that needs to get done in a harmonious, joyful manner. Do your best to feel it happening and see it unfolding in your mind's eye.

Visioning Exercise Variation #2:

Select an important event or activity you have coming up in the future. Follow the same guidelines for the original visioning exercise, but rather than focusing on creating the ideal life,

focus on creating the ideal experience of this event. Try your
best to keep your vision focused on your experience. See yourself
doing whatever you will be doing in a joyful and centered way,
regardless of what may be going on around you. Do your best to
imagine yourself in the experience, and you will help "rewire"
your thought patterns in that direction.

Gaining clarity about what you want in the future takes time, even once you have mastered the visualization exercise. It is a gradual process of defining and refining as you go. While it can be hard at first to figure out what you really want in your life, it's a whole lot better than riding along in the back seat.

Now you have all the various exercises, and weekly and monthly assessments. I hope you are clear on how it all works! If you are feeling confused, there are three ways to clarify things. First is a summary of all the exercises and assessments and when to do them in Appendix B: Exercise Summary. Second is a complete set of free templates you can download at www.AppreciativeLiving.com that will walk you through the twenty-eight-day program. Finally, you can also sign up for a free twenty-eight-day program on the website, where you receive daily e-mails with everything you need to complete your exercises and assessments.

All three exercises together provide a great platform for stepping into joy. The fact that two thirds of the participants in the study continued doing some version of the exercises after twenty-eight days, and over half were still doing part of them six months later (see Appendix H: Joy Study Results Summary) tells you that they are a powerful tool. And now it's up to you.

I hope you will be inspired to give the exercises a try. The stories may have triggered new ideas in your head, but they won't change a thing in your life until you do the exercises yourself. Joy is not something you can learn from someone else. It is something you must discover for yourself, and in the next chapter I share seven secrets for staying the course.

And remember to dream big, because it's all within your reach.

11

Discipline Dos: Seven Secrets for Staying on Track

It's easy to be on autopilot. We need to
make time to stop and check in.
—*Study participant*

At the 2007 Appreciative Inquiry conference, David Cooperrider shared a conversation he had had with leadership expert Peter Drucker. Drucker had described a hypothetical scenario in which a ship was out to sea and ran into a terrible storm. As the ship was being blown all about the crew struggled to keep it righted and together. At this point in the story Drucker paused and posed a question to David: "Who is the most important person in this scenario?"

Who do you think the most important person is? Is it the captain giving orders? Is it the crew mates responsible for carrying them out? Is it the person on the lookout reading the storm and incoming waves? As David and Peter talked back and forth, Peter finally suggested, "Perhaps it is the person who designed the ship." Think about that for a moment.

This is a great analogy for our own lives. How often do we find ourselves in the heat of a storm, thrashing around, trying to find our way through? We say we have no time to design the ship and strengthen its foundation because we're too busy just trying to stay afloat. If we make time upfront to think about the design of our lives, we will ride the storms much better. In fact, we can get to the point where we learn how to avoid many of the storms altogether. The three simple exercises in this book are designed to do just that.

All right already. If you've gotten this far into the book it is likely that you have found these exercises to be important, and that you need to do them. The study participants figured this out after doing the exercises and experiencing significant changes in their lives. So why did one third of the people stop after twenty-eight days, even though they were getting good results? Why did half the people in the study quit doing the exercises after six months, but yet when asked, they said they wanted to get back to them? Sound familiar? Have you ever embarked on a journey toward something better in your life and then departed somewhere along the way? Is this not the epitome of the eternal human struggle?

We all know this stuff works, right? But the million dollar question is: "Why don't we do what we know we need to do?" (Frankly, I believe it's worth at least a million dollars because once you figure it out, abundance is just one of the many things you can create.) We're talking five minutes a day and fifteen on the weekend, so this is not about time.

Over lunch one of the study participants and I mulled this over. She said she would never have had the discipline to do the exercises consistently if she hadn't been part of a study and "had" to do them. I told her that even after seeing all these results and being immersed in it, I was not as diligent in doing the exercises as I would have liked to be, either. It was frustrating, to say the least, but fascinating at the same time. It opened up a whole new inquiry for me. I couldn't even go to my bookshelf for this one. I had to buy a whole new series of books.

In this chapter I'll share the best practices that others have used to reach success. Consider trying some of them yourself. Not only can they help you to complete the exercises, but they also can help you in any area of your life where you need more discipline to make change.

I have found seven different ways to make yourself do what you know you need to do. I'm sure there are more, but there are enough here for you to find at least two or three that fit your style. I've summarized them for easy reference in Appendix F.

1. Create Positive Rituals

In *The Power of Full Engagement*, Jim Loehr and Tony Schwartz discuss the importance and power of creating rituals to achieve what you want. They define a ritual as a behavior you do that becomes automatic over time.[47] Each of us has rituals we perform automatically, such as brushing our teeth, showering, or any number of tasks we can easily do on autopilot. They discuss how we can create positive rituals to help instill positive changes in our lives:

> *Look at any part of your life in which you are consistently effective and you will find that certain habits help make that possible. If you eat in a healthy way, it is probably because you*

have built routines around the food you buy and what you are
willing to order at restaurants ... If you are closely connected
to your spouse and your children, you probably have rituals
around spending time with them ... Creating positive rituals is
the most powerful means we have found to effectively manage
energy in the service of full engagement.[48]

Loehr and Schwartz explain that one of the best ways to ensure success with personal change is to create positive rituals. The key to doing this effectively is to specify ahead of time just when, where, and how we will do the positive activity. They mention a number of fascinating studies supporting this concept. This is one concerning drug addiction:

As part of the effort to help [drug addicts] find employment
post-rehabilitation, one group was asked to commit to writing
a short resume before 5:00 p.m. on a particular day. Not a single
one succeeded. A second group was asked to complete the same
task, but also to say exactly when and where they would write
the resume. Eighty percent of that group succeeded.[49]

In another study that attempted to get college students to join an exercise program, participation increased from 39 percent to a whopping 91 percent when the students were asked to designate when and where they intended to exercise. Loehr and Schwartz go on to say that similar results were observed in helping people develop healthy eating habits:

Participants proved far more likely to eat healthy, low calo-
rie foods when they were asked in advance to specify precisely

what they intended to eat for each of their meals during the day,
rather than using their energy to resist eating certain foods all
day long.[50]

We can create and sustain positive rituals by determining in advance when, where, and how we will do the exercises. Several participants figured this out on their own, and described the rituals they created to help themselves keep up with the exercises:

Having the discipline of sitting down with a lined sheet of
paper (I use a spiral notebook) and writing the same thing, the
same way every day, with the same pen is the rigor that holds
me. This ritual anchors my day.

I have incorporated writing in my joy journal with my
morning tea ritual. I take that time in the peace of the morning
to center myself around what I'm grateful for and how I can
invite more joy into my life.

It is easier to incorporate the exercises into an existing ritual such as regular tea time or reading the morning paper rather than trying to create an entirely new ritual. If you have already established a habit for doing one activity, it is easier to tack on an extra five minutes than to create a separate new habit.

Several participants found that using a dedicated notebook was part of the ritual for them, so this may be something you want to consider.

I started with a notebook I had been carrying around. The
study kicked off, and I opened the notebook and started writing

wherever I was sitting. I then started intentionally carrying it outside with my coffee, where I could experience the beauty outside of the house and sunflowers, etc.

I did the exercises in a little moleskin notebook. . . . They have a wonderful feel about them. When I see the notebook, it's like a physical reminder to do the exercises.

Do the exercises in whatever way works best for you. You could try incorporating them into your regular morning routine. For example, you might consider keeping a journal by the bathroom sink near your toothbrush. Seeing the journal could act as a trigger for you to think of what to put on your appreciation list while you brush. You could then write your items down when you are done and take thirty seconds to close your eyes at the sink and feel your gratitude. Or when you step into the shower or put on your clothes you could reflect on the daily question and once you are done you could write down your response. The visioning exercise could be added on to the end of some routine you perform weekly, such as cutting your nails.

While this borders on multitasking, it can be an effective way of incorporating the exercises into your existing routine. While sitting down for five minutes and focusing exclusively on the exercises is better, it is only better if you actually do it. If you find you're having trouble getting to the exercises, tying them into an existing routine such as the ones suggested might work for you.

Some people take a specific time of day to look at their e-mail, so I developed a program at www.AppreciativeLiving.com that sends you daily e-mails with everything you need to do the exercises and assessments. This is another way of incorporating them into an existing ritual.

You can also use the exercises to help deal with rituals you'd like to change, as this person discovered:

> *Five p.m. is a dangerous time for me. I want to grab a*
> *glass of wine and a snack. I want to end the day and move*
> *into relaxation mode. So I did the exercises at 5 p.m. It short-*
> *circuited or delayed it.*

Many participants found it helpful to write down exactly where, when, and how they would do the exercises. As noted before, studies show this type of practice dramatically increases the likelihood you will follow through.

2. Track Your Results

It has been shown that people who track their results are 50 percent more likely to make progress than those who don't.[51] This is quite a significant difference, so it is definitely worth considering. In the previous chapters, I gave two different subjective evaluations you can use to determine your progress and get the most out of the exercises. One is the weekly assessment, which consists of two questions and is done in lieu of the daily exercises once a week. The second is the monthly assessment, which is done in place of the visioning exercise once a month. Both are summarized in Appendix B: Exercise Summary.

These assessments help you see your progress, which, as I explained in the Positive Principle, can be difficult to do. The upward trend toward happiness can be hard to discern while you are in the throes of the inevitable ups and downs of life. By periodically reflecting on your overall experience, you can notice the ways in which you are making progress, and perceived success will help motivate you to continue the journey. I urge you to do this so you can stay on track.

I suggest that you measure your progress on a numerical scale no more than two or three times a year. My stockbroker told me never to check my investments on a daily basis, since fluctuations are inevitable. The same is true of joy. Although I know a lot of people love numerical scales, I am not a huge fan of them, as it is unrealistic to think a wildly subjective concept like joy can be given a numerical value. Magazine articles and books are replete with short tests you can take to determine everything from how happy you are to what kind of dog you should own. And so even though I believe you are better off determining your progress from the inside, measurement tools can have some value. I'll share with you the one I prefer.

There are a variety of happiness assessments available and new and better ones are continually being created. I recommend the Oxford Happiness Questionnaire, which is included in Appendix E: Oxford Happiness Questionnaire. You can also take this assessment for free at www.AppreciativeLiving.com. This questionnaire provides a reasonably comprehensive evaluation of happiness, which is helpful for long-term comparison. As I mentioned before, I would not take this or any other numerical assessment more than a couple of times a year, but would continue to do the subjective evaluations on a regular basis.

There are two more ways you might consider the use of tracking with the exercises. First, create a checklist or spreadsheet and check it off each day after you do the exercises. Keep it somewhere you will see it regularly. Second, periodically review what you've written in your journal or wherever you have documented the exercises. It's interesting to see how your thinking changes over time and can help provide a sense of progress.

3. Reward Your Success

The third way you can help keep yourself on track is by using rewards. Research shows that when we experience the pleasure of a reward after doing a new activity, our brain actually secretes chemical neurotransmitters that reinforce the changes we just made.[52] Some of the new learning tools developed by neuroscientists include a reward system that activates once you attain a certain level of skill. We can use this concept to help reinforce change as well. The reward doesn't have to be anything fancy, just something that brings pleasure.

Besides, who couldn't use a little more fun? Begin by making a list of things you enjoy, and then select one of them at the beginning of the week you will use as your reward. Use this to motivate yourself to do the exercises and to reinforce your success at the end of the week. You can put anything on your list, from a special hobby or coffee with a friend, to a candlelight bubble bath or a round of golf. You can also plan mini rewards every day or so to keep you motivated throughout the week. Make a list of smaller, simpler items for this list, such as enjoying a special cup of tea, listening to music you love, or spending a few minutes with your pet.

Rewards are win-win-win, because they get you to think about what brings you joy, motivate you to do the exercises, and then reinforce your new thought patterns all at the same time. Give rewards a try.

4. Create Novelty

There is a certain excitement and aliveness that comes when we first do something new or visit a place we have never been. It is a stimulating period, and we find ourselves immersed in the new experience, intrigued with the different way of being and doing. The longer we stay in the new place, the less enthralling it all becomes, and eventually we adapt to it. At this point the novelty is gone, and so is the excitement and freshness of the experience. Dan Gilbert explains:

> *When we have an experience . . . we quickly begin to adapt to it, and the experience yields less pleasure each time. Psychologists call this habituation, economists call it declining marginal utility, and the rest of us call it marriage.*[53]

Jokes aside, the point is that anything we do for an extended period of time eventually loses its oomph. We need to shake things up and shift them around to keep them interesting and engaging. The same is true of the joy exercises. In Appendix B, I provide two modifications of each exercise to help keep them fresh.

I suggest you get a solid grounding in the exercises before you start changing them. I would do them exactly as written for at least twenty-eight days, but ideally for several months. Then you can begin experimenting if you like. Some people will be content to do them as written for months and months, while others who are not as routine or structured will be ready for change much sooner.

Some people, like me, require a lot more novelty than others. I have never stayed in any job more than three years, and am notorious for six-month jaunts into what appear as strange tangents to the outside world. I mix things up tremendously with my practices, doing everything from five-minute visualizations before dinner parties, to one-hour detailed interludes of my dream life on long car rides. There are days I write for twenty minutes on what I appreciate, and times I stop and think of one good thing about a situation I'm about to face. I will go for days without intentionally asking an appreciative question, and then I will be mindful of my every conversation and spend dedicated time reflecting on many questions. This is more novelty than most people need, but for other change addicts out there, mixing things up will give you a sense of the possibilities. In the next chapter I talk more about using the exercises in the long term, including how to vary them.

Mix it up enough to keep it interesting, but make sure you are hitting each of the three exercises on some type of regular basis. There is a synergy among them that accelerates the change process, so it's helpful to work them all at the same time. The bottom line is that if the exercises start feeling a bit stale, it's time to shake it up.

5. Get Inspired

The fifth way to stay the course is through inspiration, which I like to distinguish from motivation. Both create a strong internal desire or drive to make a change, but inspiration comes from a distinctly positive source. Motivation can come from either.

Most of us are motivated or inspired in the beginning when we start something new, whether it's a new diet, a new class, or a new home improvement project. We get all excited in the beginning and dive in with the best of intentions. Then something happens along the way, our desire drops off, and our well-intentioned efforts follow right along with it.

Before we look at why the excitement level drops off, let's look at where the desire for change came from in the first place. I see motivation as having two distinct sources: positive or negative. We tend to act either from negative emotion, like fear or pain, or from positive emotion, like excitement or hope. Where we start is important, because one emotion will give us a lot more momentum than the other. And you can already guess which one is which.

There is a fair amount of research that suggests negative emotion is not an effective long-term motivator for change. I prefer to think of it as a stimulus or kick in the pants. It gets us going, but after a relatively brief period it ceases to motivate us, and our best intentions cease right along with it. In *Get Out of Your Own Way*, Robert Cooper describes a clinical trial done by Dr. Dean Ornish with 333 patients with severely clogged arteries that demonstrates this idea:

> *All these years, physicians had been trying to motivate patients with facts about their desperate straits or with the outright fear of death, and it wasn't working. For a week or so after a heart attack or bypass surgery, patients were scared enough to do whatever their doctors said. But death was too daunting to*

think about, so their denial or stonewalling would increase, and they'd revert to their old habits and stay there, unchanged.[54]

Negative emotion is not an effective source for long-term motivation, but it is still one of the most common motivating factors. When our life feels incredibly wonderful and perfect, that is not generally the time we think to ourselves, "Gee, I think I'll go to the bookstore and get a few books on joy, and then start a major personal growth program." It's when we're down and out that we tend to seek these kinds of things. Negative emotions are not going away any time soon, and they are in fact wonderful gifts for change. We just need to learn how to work with them.

The secret is in learning to turn the pain and fear of the negative emotion into hope and inspiration for change. It's learning to see the improvement that is needed, but rather than *moving away* from fear or pain, you *move toward* what you want. Is any of this sounding familiar?

We all know intuitively that when we feel inspired to do something, it is easy to make it happen. The question is, "How do you create the inspiration?" Now we've come full circle. Inspiration can be another word for joy.

One way to build inspiration is to create a future image so compelling that everything in you wants to make it happen. A compelling vision will sustain you long after fear loses its ability to motivate. That's essentially what Dean Ornish did with the heart patients in the clinical trial mentioned above:

Ornish changed the entire context of change, helping each patient see a new vision of the joy of living, convincing them

*they could feel better and enjoy an unprecedented richness
of living, not just hang on a little longer. Not just convincing
them—showing them how they could once again enjoy the things
that make daily life joyful, like getting slim and strong again,
making love, or even gardening or taking long strolls without the
pain caused by their disease. "Joy is a more powerful motivator
than fear," he says.*[55]

I couldn't have said it better myself. One of the best ways to get
yourself inspired to do the exercises is to do the exercises! The
second visioning exercise in particular helps you continue to
connect to your inspiration. Make your image of your ideal,
joy-filled life as real and detailed as possible, as if it is actually
happening right now. The more authentic you make it, the more
powerful a force for change it will be. And when you feel yourself
slacking off on the exercises, return to your vision of the life of
your dreams and reengage with it. Make it come alive again and
reconnect to the emotion. Find your inspiration in your dreams
of the future and let it grab your heart. Then trust your heart to
lead you where your head cannot. Use visualization as your personal bridge to inspiration.

6. Partner with Someone or Join a Group

The sixth tip for increasing your chance of success with the
exercises is finding a partner or buddy to do them with, or joining a group. There are multiple benefits to joining with others
in making change; the WeightWatchers program is one of the

most well-known. Studies show that people who attend weekly meetings are more successful in losing weight than those who don't.[56] The accountability you have to a program or partner helps you stay on track, and for those socialites out there, it's just plain more fun. Here are two different ways you can do the exercises with others:

1. Find a friend who wants to do the exercises, and make a commitment to meet, call, or e-mail each week to check in on how each of you are doing.
2. Join an Appreciative Living Learning Circle through my website at www.AppreciativeLiving.com.

Not only does working with others increase your chances of sticking with the program, it also accelerates your results as you learn with them.

7. Do It Anyway

This last tip is not profound, but it needs to be said. Sometimes you just have to make it happen. I can't tell you how many times I drag myself to the gym when there are about twelve hundred other things I'd rather be doing. There are days you just don't feel like it, and sometimes you have to bite the bullet and do it anyway. This tip certainly isn't going to motivate you for the long haul, but it's worth remembering for those days when your excuses cloud your vision.

In summary, there are seven ways you can increase your discipline in following through with the exercises:

7 Secrets for Staying on Track

1. Create Positive Rituals
2. Track Your Results
3. Reward Your Success
4. Create Novelty
5. Get Inspired
6. Partner with Someone or Join a Group
7. Do It, Anyway

The seven ways are also listed with a brief summary in Appendix F: Seven Discipline Dos Summary. Apply the ones that fit for you, and if none of them work, just do the exercises anyway. And when you're really lost in excuse land, remember one of my favorite quotes: "You always have time for the things you put first."

12

Bliss, Anyone? The Five Stages of Deliberate Change

I've continued to do the exercises pretty much every day.
It just doesn't feel like I'm aligned if I don't.
—Study participant

Here's where it all comes together. In this chapter I'm going to talk about life in the joy lane and where my journey has led. From my experience I have identified five stages we go through during significant personal changes. In this chapter I'll share those five stages and what you can expect at each one, to give you a sense of the larger overall journey. I will also show you how you can use the exercises to make any change you want in your life. I'd like to share here my story of personal significant change.

Several years ago on a cold, rainy Monday morning, I got up at 5:45 a.m. as usual to get my children ready for school. After getting book bags and lunches packed, and everyone dressed and fed, I loaded the car for our one-hour commute. We stopped along the way to pick up one more child and headed into the rainy morning. The drizzly weather added another fifteen minutes onto the drive, and we just barely made it through the school drop-off line before they closed it down.

After I let the kids off I headed to the nearest coffee shop for my coveted two hours and forty-seven minutes of alone time in which I did my writing. Today it would be shortened by fifteen minutes, which was a big deal in my jam-packed world. I had developed an efficient routine once I got to the coffee shop, where I set up my dinosaur computer on a table and then ordered coffee while it took an eternity to boot up. By the time I got back with caffeine in hand the computer was ready to go, and I got right down to business and typed away for every second I had. When my time was up, I went back to pick up my son from his half day at school. My son ate his lunch in the car while I drove thirty minutes back home, stopping at the post office and two different stores to pick up groceries and prescriptions along the way. After I got home and unloaded the car, checked the mail, threw in a load of laundry, vacuumed the family room, and took something out of the freezer for dinner, my son and I snuggled together on the couch for a few moments. He was engrossed in the purple dinosaur Barney and I was engrossed in the back of my eyelids. Then it was off to pick up my daughter and return home for an important call I had late that afternoon.

The kids went outside to play while I got on the phone, and the call ended up going much longer than I anticipated. While the other person was talking, I looked up at the clock and realized I needed to leave in fifteen minutes for a speaking engagement. I was not dressed yet, the kids were still outside playing, and my husband was nowhere in sight. I panicked and worked my way off the call, and then the doorbell rang. It was the two little neighbor girls, and I decided as I ran to the door that whatever they wanted would have to wait, or so I thought. I changed my mind quickly when they turned and pointed to the edge of our yard, where my son was wallowing in a small pile of mud like an overheated farm animal. Needless to say, I had to intervene.

Right about this time Jon pulled in the driveway and I cleverly turned it all over to him. I managed to make it to the speaking engagement on time, did my thing, and arrived back home around 10:30 p.m. to go to bed and get up and do it all over again.

This was a typical day in my typical life about three years ago—lots of action, lots of drama, and lots of craziness. It was full of jam-packed schedules and near-misses, but in the end I always managed to pull everything off. I had lots of great stories for cocktail parties, but who am I kidding, I haven't seen a cocktail party since the kids were born! It made great conversation with the neighbor ladies and justified my existence as a stay-at-home mom to Jon. We would trade stories about whose day was crazier, and compete for who got the least sleep. He would say things like, "I drove three hundred miles and the customer cancelled the meeting so I had to turn around and drive three hundred miles back home." I would counter with, "Yeah, well, I forgot that the kids had a field trip today and they didn't have bagged lunches, so I had to rush out after car pool drop-off and bring the lunches back before they left, and I pulled in right as the cars were pulling out, and then...." On it would go. Drama, drama, drama. I trumped him the day I got so busy and confused I missed picking the kids up from school. Touché.

Stage 1: Awareness

Somewhere in the midst of the craziness, I came face-to-face with the stark realization that I was addicted to drama. As I mentioned earlier, we all have our own unique joy path, and although my life had gotten significantly better, there was still a lot of crazy activity. One of the most important things the exercises do is allow you to stop for a moment and take a serious look at your life. They force you to get honest about what is and isn't working and to do something about it, or at least accept responsibility for what's going on. I call this stage 1 of the joy journey: Awareness, the realization that there is a part of your life that is not bringing you joy. This stage can go on indefinitely if you do not deliberately move to stage 2.

Stage 2: Commitment

About six months after the realization that there was more craziness in my life than I wanted, I formally entered stage 2. I made a decision to do something about the situation. Until this point I was aware of the drama, but since I did nothing to intervene, it continued. I was now actively ready to change. Stage 2 began as I committed to making a shift.

I knew from the Poetic Principle that I had to choose what I wanted more of—and not less of—in order to create it. I was certain about what I did *not* want: the drama and struggle. So I spent some time getting clearer about what I did want, and decided it was to have life flow smoothly and easily. The expression that most captured it for me was "to have things just fall in my lap." I could feel the stress flow right out of my body as I said this.

Stage 3: Action

Once I committed to create more ease in my life, I entered stage 3. It was time to do something about the situation. I began intentionally looking for ways to shift my thinking toward the easy road. I took the first appreciation exercise and started noticing anything that went smoothly and easily during the day, even if it was something small. Every once in a while I would write it down, but usually I just made a mental note to look for it. I also went out and bought a button at an office supply store that spews out a nasal rendition of "that was easy" when hit. I happily smacked it whenever something went my way. My son grew particularly fond of the button, and occasionally it would disappear and I'd hear it go off from upstairs in his room. It was a fun way to reinforce the belief I was trying to adopt that things could be easy.

I also became very aware of my conversations. I began by simply noticing the way I talked about my life. As people would ask me how things were going, in the beginning I found myself saying things like "It's out of control" and "Just crazy." I heard how my language and stories clearly mirrored my experience, and for several months I just became more aware.

I then took the third exercise and visualized life events flowing easily and freely, and imagined myself effortlessly going through the day. I did not get into the details of how it was going to happen, I just imagined it at a high level. Here is one of my visualizations:

My life flows so easily and smoothly it is unbelievable. I wake up every morning from a good night's sleep and glide out of bed. Things just come my way and I don't even know how it happens a lot of the time. It's amazing to live in such a state of flow and grace. Everything that needs to get done gets done, and I enjoy the process. It's like I float through my day and everything shows up to meet me. The right people appear at just the right time, and things just fall right in my lap. I end up having enough time to relax in the evenings and do things just for me. It's amazing—I just smile through it all. There is an incredible ease in everything I do, whether it's daily activities or relationships or writing or speaking or cleaning or cooking or working out or driving or having fun. Everything goes so well, I regularly sit back and just bask in appreciation for how I live. It is a dream. I can't believe how hard I used to struggle and now I just sail through. It's amazing what can happen when you let go and trust in the process of life.

I only did a few visualizations, but I really got into them. I would also think about them briefly at random times and dream about this wonderful new life. I would only take a few minutes at most to visualize, although there was one car trip where I distinctly remember gazing off and dreaming for probably a half hour or more. (No, I was not driving.)

The last thing I did in stage 3 was to modify the daily question to "What one thing could I do today, no matter how small, to make my life easier and more joyful?" I found two big areas for change as I answered this question. The first was in getting more organized, and the other was pulling nonessential items off my to-do list. The latter one was a doozey. Before committing to anything, I held it up to the litmus test of whether or not it would make my life easier and/or more joyful. If the activity did not pass, most of the time I did not do it. A good chunk of activities went by the wayside, though there were a few exceptions.

Stage 4: Acclimation

I have to tell you, it was a real struggle giving up the drama. (See how ingrained it was? I even struggled to give up the struggle!) As things started getting a bit easier, I found myself feeling a little lost, believe it or not. It was a weird experience. As I began to lose the drama, it felt like I was losing a part of my identity. I found myself clamoring for something to say when Jon would come home. Rather than blurting out a can-you-top-this story, I would give a mousy little report of the day's events. Jon would come in with some glamorous, exciting, dramatic event to retell and I would say something like "Gee, it was a pretty good day today . . . I got the kids off to school fine and we had a nice morning . . . and then I worked on my book and the writing flowed easily . . . I made some calls and that went well . . . Let me think, there must be something else . . . I mailed some books and there was no line . . . and there must be *something* eventful to tell you about today . . ."

The craziness was a big part of my identity story, and when it left I didn't quite know who I was. Drama had become one of the ways I justified my existence. Rather than talking about how crazy my life was, I began hesitatingly telling people in a calm voice that things were, in fact, pretty good. In stage 4 I was laying down new track as I let go of the old frenetic me and acclimated to the new, calmer one. Things got kind of quiet for a while as I got in touch with who I was underneath the drama. As my eyes opened in the stillness of the new way of being, I felt more serene, but unsettled. When the pattern of struggle subsided it left a void that begged to be filled. I was tempted to pack it back in with drama (and occasionally I still manage to do this) but over time I adjusted to this newer, easier, and more peaceful existence.

I also found myself clearing clutter out of my house at a rampant rate. I'd done this during other personal growth phases, and I'm beginning to wonder if it's a stage of its own. I call it purging, letting go of the old to make way for the new. It manifests physically for me in cleaning out my house, but it goes on mentally as well. And it probably shows up in other ways that I'm not even aware of.

Stage 5: Realization

I'm now entering stage 5. It is fascinating to watch how this process continues to unfold, but my dream of living easier is beginning to be realized. Things go smoothly more often than not, and it feels like my life has taken a whole new turn. I generally find myself in the right places at the right time and wonderful coincidences seem to pop up everywhere. It is fascinating to see how this dream has manifested. It is surprising to me that life is still exciting, but in a different way. I'm busier than ever but I generally don't get too uptight about it. I find myself inspired and energized by what goes on instead of being exhausted by it.

Occasionally I feel the panic sort of bubbling up, but when I'm in a good place I'm able to let it pass and keep my calm center. When I'm not in a good place I get snarled up and find myself feeling like my life is crazy and out of control. The good news is that I usually can get back to my calmer state in fairly short order. I'm also getting a lot more done.

I can't tell you how much smoother things are now. Clearing the drama and chaos out of my life has made space for the important things to flow easily. Even the way the publisher of this book came in was nothing short of miraculous. A gentleman in one of my audiences liked what he heard, and told me he just happened to be having lunch with a big publisher soon. I put together a short proposal for this book over the weekend, and two weeks later I got an offer from Tarcher Publishing. And here we are. I hit the Easy button ten times for that one.

Here is a summary of the five stages to changing your life, and you can also find them in Appendix G.

The Five Stages of Deliberate Change

Stage 1: Awareness: Recognizing that something in your life is not bringing joy

Stage 2: Commitment: Deciding and committing to create *more* of what you want

Stage 3: Action: Using the exercises to create what you want *more of*

Stage 4: Acclimation: Adjusting to the new and letting go of the old

Stage 5: Realization: Living into the new way of being

Lest you come to the erroneous conclusion that I have life in the bag, let me assure you I'm still very much on the journey. I still have my down periods, too, though they don't go down as far and I don't stay there nearly as long as in the past. I can't. I have too many tools now to get myself out. The funny thing is that sometimes I don't choose to use the tools. Notice the word *choose*. You can use the same process to create unhappiness as you do joy.

Occasionally I get really upset or have a bad day and just sit in the yuck and feel sorry for myself. Although I don't know why I do it, I'll just hang out in my grumpy place longer than I need to. I know I can choose to pull myself out by looking for the good, but sometimes I ignore myself and just sit in it. I remember a study where researchers gave electric shocks to baby rats from the moment they were born. After a period of time a door was opened and the rats were allowed to leave the shock room and live in other parts of the cage. They all scrambled out when given the chance and lived a peaceful rat existence in other parts of their habitat. But then a scary thing happened.

Slowly the rats started going back into the shock room and eventually every one of them returned and stayed there. It makes me wonder. A lot of my life in the past was spent in low places and sometimes when I go back there, it almost feels like coming home to an old friend. If nothing else, it's familiar. I have to say, though, I'm noticing that it's not as much fun down there as it used to be, and I'm spending less and less time visiting. I'm imagining there will come a day when it loses its appeal altogether.

We have habits in our way of thinking that we have to undo when we make changes in our lives. In learning to let go of struggle, I shifted my thinking from how everything required so much work to the ways in which life flowed easily. It was not an easy switch, and it took about eight months until it began to stick. Recent brain research suggests it takes about six months for a change to become permanent if you work at it steadily:

> *After a brief period of practice, as when we cram for a test, it is relatively easy to improve because we are likely strengthening existing synaptic connections. But we quickly forget what we've crammed—because these are easy-come, easy-go neuronal connections and are rapidly reversed. Maintaining improvement and making a skill permanent require the slow steady work that probably forms new connections . . . which in Braille readers took six months.*[57]

For all of us in the "I want it now" category, which includes me, six months can seem like an eternity. That's when you have to step back and look at how long you've been doing it the other way. You'll begin to realize that deep inside you know intuitively that big changes take time. The good news is once you make a big change, it takes a long time to undo. Like most things in life, the permanence of our habits works for us and against us. We can use this to our advantage—by consistently doing the exercises we deliberately create more positive thinking patterns.

Let's not forget about the short-term benefits. While it's great to get to the point where our new behaviors become part of our automatic thinking, there is a lot to be enjoyed along the way. As I mentioned earlier, participants in the study got significantly happier in twenty-eight days, and many reported noticing a difference in even just a few days. The exercises were also an effective tool for some people in dealing with difficulties that came their way:

> *I had a bad day at work. I came home and did the exercises and the whole day disappeared. I felt so much better and was actually looking forward to the next day.*

> *There was one day where everyone was coming down on me. I felt like the whole world was caving in. I really looked forward to the next morning and having that time to reflect. It put my mind into a much more positive state . . . It really cleared my mind and helped me to get through a very, very stressful time.*

> *I suspect that I will continue to do the daily exercises into the future. They didn't take much time, and they were very help-ful in preventing me from sliding toward the dark side of the force ("Luke, the dark side of the force is very powerful!") during some difficult times in my life.*

The other good news is that it takes a relatively short time to begin creating more happiness. While investing more time will likely increase your results, you can get a lot of benefit from the exercises with only five minutes a day and fifteen minutes on the weekends. I like to vary it up a bit; for example, I might do a full thirty minutes of appreciation or visioning one day, and then not do it again for a week. In the end, I average about an hour a week working on some version of the exercises. Some weeks it's more, some less.

A fair amount of these changes have become part of my automatic thinking processes. For example, my initial reaction in a difficult situation is typically to trust that it will all work out, and to look for what's good. This was far from the case in the beginning of my journey. I am also much more aware of my conversations now, both with myself and others; this allows me to be much more deliberate about where my stories are headed.

But again, the point is that meaningful changes do not have to take a lot of time. Recent studies show that small time investments can have big benefits in the area of physical exercise as well. In the past, experts suggested that adults exercise for thirty to sixty minutes per day[58] in order to get results, but recent research shows that significant improvements can be had with as little as ten minutes of exercise a day.[59] While more is better, less can be good enough.

The last five years of my joy journey have been intensely focused on the Appreciative Living principles, which has led me to make changes in every area of my life, to the point that I hardly recognize it anymore. I knew things had changed radically when two different people recently described me as laid back! I consider this quite a statement, as I was voted either one of the most intense or serious people in my MBA graduating class. The fact that a professor had to call 911 after I passed out from exhaustion and dehydration while doing a class presentation might have had something to do with it. My life at that time was defined by intense activity, excitement, and drama. And now, well, it looks a lot different.

Now one of my favorite things to do is to sit outside in my driveway on a lawn chair in the early evening. I watch my children run and play with a carefree joy I recall from my own past, while in the back of my mind I know the teenage years are just around the corner. Jon and I talk about how someday we'd like to add a screened-in porch so we don't have to deal with bugs and drag chairs in and out, but I'm smart enough now to know it won't make us any happier. I always set up at least one extra lawn chair in the driveway, sometimes two, and inevitably a neighbor or passerby will find their way there. If it's a Friday evening we might end up with eight or ten different people, and sometimes we keep on talking until it's so late we order pizza for dinner and let the kids stay up to catch frogs with flashlights. We talk and laugh about the week and life and nothing in particular. I have a feeling I will look back on these evenings as some of my favorites.

Does joy make you boring? Perhaps it does in some ways. I certainly don't need all the stimulation and excitement that I used to need in the past. I find it pretty easy to enjoy whatever happens to be going on, which at this stage of life in suburbia with two young children is not all that much. At the same time, I can be packed in half an hour if anyone would like to send me on an exotic trip. It's not that I don't *want* to do exciting things anymore; it's that I don't *need* to do them to be happy. I'm beginning to get that idea of detachment.

The way I frame situations and respond to them has changed significantly, and the big things no longer seem like big things. I became particularly aware of this recently when I coasted through a situation that would have completely unraveled me before.

It was Saturday morning and I was looking forward to going for a massage that Jon had given me for Christmas. I decided to run a few errands on the way there, which required me to load up my passenger seat with items for the bank, post office, and Goodwill community center. The first stop I made was to the bank, and when I got there I dug through the pile to find the bank envelope. It had about $600 worth of checks and cash that were all clipped together, signed, and ready to go. I kept digging and digging, and then I dug some more. I couldn't find it. I knew I had put it in the car, but I just couldn't find it. My heart started beating a little faster, but nothing I would call panic. I kept looking. It wasn't there.

I called Jon and asked him to look around at home. He looked in the house, the garage, the street, and everyplace I had been. By the time he called back to say he couldn't find it, I had gone through everything in my car twice. I looked at the clock and it was time to drive to my massage.

Let me stop the story and tell you what would have been going on in my head in the past at this point. I would have been thinking in expletives like "Where the $!@%&$# did the money go? What the %$#@% happened to it! What if someone stole it? It's all cash and the checks are signed! How the &^%$# did this happen?"

I would have then called and cancelled my massage, retraced my steps, and done everything conceivable under the sky to try to find the money. Panic, fear, and drama would have been the order of the day. Now let me tell you what actually happened.

I sat in my car with the realization that I possibly might have just lost $600, and it was in someone else's hands. My next thought was that everything is in divine order, and whoever had the money must have needed it more than I did. While $600 is a lot of money, it's not like I would go hungry or be unable to pay the mortgage if I lost it. I then imagined some downtrodden person suddenly finding this windfall of money and jumping for joy over his good fortune. (I have to admit I did stereotype and imagine it was a man.) It put a smile on my face for a moment to realize I may have just made someone's entire day or even month.

This story may sound absurd to you, and frankly it's sounding absurd to me as I write it. But that's honestly what went through my mind, and it allowed me to stay calm and composed in the midst of the situation. In this centered place I was able to think rationally about what had happened and I concluded the money could only be in one of three places: my car or my house, or it had gotten stuck in my car door and fallen out along the way. Based on this analysis, I made a decision that seemed reasonable. I called the massage person and said I would be fifteen minutes late, and then I retraced my path with the car to see if the money had fallen out anywhere along the way. I didn't find it, so I went to my massage and decided I'd look again in the car and house when I got home.

I thoroughly enjoyed the massage and did not spend a minute worrying about the money. I even forgot about it on the way home as I listened to music and enjoyed the beautiful weather. When I got home, Jon pulled the car apart, and sure enough he found the money. It had slipped down between the two front seats and had lodged behind one of the seat motors.

This situation could have ruined my entire morning and afternoon, but as it turns out it only cost me a few moments of heightened anxiety. It has taken me a lot of years to get there, but I have to tell you it has been worth it. I also have to tell you I still have more work to do.

That same afternoon upon returning home and finding the money, my son started running a fever and I got out a thermometer I had recently purchased. It was wrapped in one of those thick clear plastic packages that appear to be vacuum sealed together. Jon is a plastics engineer and he tells me they are sonic welded, but I call it %$#@* welded. I started trying to break into the thing, and it wasn't pretty. When I get mad I make these grunting noises and I use the "S" word, which in our family is "stupid." I could not get the "S" thing open, because they use this "S" packaging method and I ended up cutting my "S" finger in the process. Jon took over at the sight of blood and cut it open with a utility knife while I immediately got on the phone to call the 800 number on the back of the package to "share my concerns." After pushing phone buttons through four different menu options I finally got a message saying, "Our offices are now closed." You should have heard the noise I made at that point.

While I handled the missing $600 like a pro, I lost it over thermometer packaging the very same day. You don't want to be within earshot of me when the computer acts up, either. So, yes, I still have work to do on the eternal upward journey to joy, and I'm sure I always will. But at least now I have a simple set of exercises to get me on the path—that is, when I *choose* to use them.

I hope you will choose to do the exercises and find your own path to joy. As you embark on the journey, you can expect to go through five stages each time you work a new area of personal change. There will always be new challenges, and each one is a special gift for your own learning that will ultimately bring you greater happiness. Stay the course by doing the exercises regularly and you will discover your own key to joy.

One participant summarized it beautifully:

Lines from the Eagles song "Already Gone" express suc-
cinctly what would take me two dozen paragraphs to say: "So

*often times it happens that we live our lives in chains, and we
never even know we have the key."*

We live our lives in chains, thinking the lottery or the new job
or the perfect relationship will make us happier, and we never
even know we have the key right now, in this moment. Well, now
you know. With the three simple exercises in this book you can
find your inner key and create a life beyond your wildest
dreams. And remember, *it's all about joy.*

Peace and blessings to every precious one of you. May you
go in joy, ever upward.

APPENDICES

What Is Appreciative Inquiry?

Appreciative Inquiry (AI) was first conceptualized at Case Western Reserve University in 1980 by doctoral student David Cooperrider and his thesis adviser, Suresh Srivastva.[60] Jane Watkins and Bernard Mohr provide a beautifully detailed history of the beginnings of AI in their book *Appreciative Inquiry: Change at the Speed of Imagination*.[61] They explain how AI began as a theory-building process and eventually evolved into the organizational change philosophy it is today.

In *The Power of Appreciative Inquiry*, AI consultants Diana Whitney and Amanda Trosten-Bloom state that "Appreciative Inquiry is the study and exploration of what gives life to human systems when they function at their best."[62] It is a positive, strength-based approach to change that includes cocreating inspiring images of what we want, and building on positive aspects to make them happen. It means becoming more aware of our internal and external dialogues and intentionally shifting them to focus on what we want more of. It unleashes the positive potential within people and situations through attention and focus on the positive core. It suggests we build on our strengths, successes, and best practices to achieve our greatest hopes and dreams. AI is all this and more.

There are eight assumptions in Appreciative Inquiry:[63]

1. In every society, organization, or group, something works.
2. What we focus on becomes our reality.
3. Reality is created in the moment, and there are multiple realities.
4. The act of asking questions of an organization or group influences the group in some way.
5. People have more confidence and comfort to journey to the future (the unknown) when they carry forward parts of the past (the known).
6. If we carry parts of the past forward, they should be what is best about the past.
7. It is important to value differences.
8. The language we use creates our reality.

AI is a living, organic concept that continuously emerges and grows with new learning and information. Appreciative Living is the simple act of applying Appreciative Inquiry to everyday life. For further information on Appreciative Inquiry, including articles, case studies, conferences, consultants, and more, visit the AI Commons website http://appreciativeinquiry.case.edu.

Exercise Summary

*Templates for the exercises and assessments in
this book are available as free downloads at:
www.AppreciativeLiving.com*

*You can also sign up for a free twenty-eight-day program
to receive daily e-mails with everything you
need to complete your exercises and assessments.*

Summary of the 28-Day Program

Exercises:

- Do the Appreciation List once a day
- Do the Daily Question Exercise once a day
- Do the Visioning Exercise once a week

Assessments:

- Before doing any of the exercises, first take the Oxford
  Happiness Questionnaire in Appendix E to establish
  your baseline level of happiness. You can take this
  assessment every six months or so if you wish to get a
  sense of your overall progress.

- Once a week do the weekly assessment in place of the two daily exercises.
- Once a month, do the monthly assessment in place of the visioning exercise.

Considerations:

- If you become bored with the exercises, try one of the variations listed on pages 166 to 168. Do the exercises for at least twenty-eight days, or ideally several months before doing the variations.
- If you are struggling with the visioning exercise, try one of the bridge exercises. Continue to return to the visioning exercise until you are able to do it.

Exercises

Daily Appreciation List:

Each morning, take a minute to get comfortable and relaxed. Get out your preferred means of expression, whether it's a pen and paper, journal, or computer. Write the date at the top, and list three things for which you are grateful. Then take thirty seconds to close your eyes and really focus on and feel your appreciation for each one. Choose three different things each time you do this exercise.

Daily Question Exercise:

Each morning, after you have done the Appreciation List, take two to three minutes to reflect on your answer to the following question and write it down: "What one thing could I do today, no matter how small, that would increase my joy?"

Weekly Visioning Exercise:

Once a week, take fifteen to twenty minutes to do the following: Get out your preferred means of documentation, whether it's a pen and paper, journal, or computer. Begin by getting yourself comfortable and feeling as good as you can. You might want to put on inspiring music, look at pictures that make you feel happy, or play with your pets. Or you can do the daily exercises to move into a place of good feeling. Write the date at the top of your paper, along with this statement: "This is my ideal, joy-filled life." Pretend that a miracle occurred and your perfect, ideal, joy-filled life manifested right now before your eyes. Write down every glorious piece you can imagine about what this ideal life looks like at the highest level. You only have fifteen minutes, so you have to keep the vision big. How is your health? Your career? Your relationships? Your home? List the ideas as they stream through your mind. Let your deepest hopes and desires come forth and dream big about your perfect, happy life. Pretend it is really happening now, and feel the joy inside of you as you write.

Here is one example:

I love my life. I get up each morning, feeling well-rested, energized, and excited to start the day. I can hardly wait to begin my work, where I feel so fulfilled and inspired that it doesn't even feel right to call it work. It is more like a calling—a passion. I feel like I am changing the world in a meaningful and

*wonderful way. And my relationships are extraordinary.
I have so many friends and family members that I love, it
is a joy to be alive. My children are so beautiful—like small
miracles. We are incredibly close and I thoroughly enjoy the
time we spend together. I learn so much from them and enjoy
them more the older they get. My husband and I are closer
than ever, and when I think our relationship can't get any better,
it does. I just love the feeling we have created in our home as
well. It is so peaceful and serene, like an oasis from the busyness
of life. My physical and mental health is extraordinary, too. I
enjoy the activities I do to keep myself in shape and feel much
younger than my age would suggest. I've really come to love and
accept my body in the aging process and enjoy the advantages of
growing older. We regularly take amazing vacations that are fun
and rejuvenating, and the part that I just can't get over is how
fun my life is! I laugh constantly, and find humor in everything.
I am so grateful to be alive and living a life beyond my wildest
dreams.*

(For additional examples, visit www.AppreciativeLiving.com.)

Assessments

Oxford Happiness Questionnaire: See Appendix E.

5-Minute Weekly Assessment: (Do in place of Appreciation List and Daily Question)

Answer these questions:

1. What two things did you learn from doing the exercises this week?
2. How was your week better because you did them?

15-Minute Monthly Assessment: (Do in place of Weekly Visioning)

Answer these questions:

1. What is working really well in your exercise routine that you'd like to build upon or continue?
2. What changes could you make, no matter how small, that would make your experience more effective, interesting, or enjoyable?
3. Answer at least one of the following questions:
   - What three to five things are currently bringing you the most joy?
   - What are you wondering or curious about at this stage of your journey?
   - How is your life getting better?
   - What has surprised you in doing the exercises?
   - Think of a situation you handled particularly well. What did you do that made it a success and what can you apply from this, going forward?

- As you reflect on your overall life vision, pick one part in particular that you are excited about. What is one thing you can do next month to move you forward in this area?

Exercise Variations

Appreciation List Variation #1:

Rather than writing a list, write a whole rambling page on someone in your life now and what you appreciate about that person. When you are done, consider giving it to him or her. I can't think of a better birthday present.

Appreciation List Variation #2:

Pick a relatively short word for the day that suggests something you appreciate, such as joy, rain, cat, or phone, and make an acrostic gratitude list. Write out the letters vertically and then list one thing you are grateful for that begins with the letter. It looks like this:

J—**J**on (my husband)
O—**O**reo cookies
Y—**Y**ellow sunshine

Feel free to be liberal and creative with your ideas so you don't waste a lot of time trying to come up with the perfect word. Afterward, close your eyes and take thirty seconds to feel the gratitude for each one. Remember that whatever you focus on grows, so I would not list something like Oreo cookies unless I wanted that to be part of my experience shortly!

Daily Question Variation #1

Vary the daily question as follows: "What one thing can I do, no matter how small, to move me in the direction of _____?" (Fill in the blank with whatever you want more of in your life, such as better health, greater abundance, or more loving relationships.)

Daily Question Variation #2

Vary the daily question as follows: "What one thing can I do today, no matter how small, to shift my attention to _____?" (Fill in the blank with whatever you want more of in your life, such as better health, greater abundance, or more loving relationships.)

Visioning Exercise Variation #1:

Perform the original visualization exercise once a month to keep your big picture going, but do mini five-minute visualizations twice a week as follows: Close your eyes and get comfortable, and think about your day ahead. Imagine it unfolding joyfully. See yourself going through the motions of each of your activities in a happy, peaceful manner. Notice how easily you flow from one thing to the next, and see yourself engaging with others in a kind and loving way. Observe everything getting done that needs to get done in a harmonious, joyful manner. Do your best to feel it happening and see it unfolding in your mind's eye.

Visioning Exercise Variation #2

Select an important event or activity you have coming up in the future. Follow the same guidelines for the original visioning exercise, but rather than focusing on creating the ideal life, focus on creating the ideal experience of this event. Try your best to keep your vision focused on your experience. See yourself doing whatever you will be doing in a joyful and centered way, regardless of what may be going on around you. Do your best to imagine yourself in the experience, and you will help rewire your thought patterns in that direction.

Visioning Bridge Exercises

Try one of these exercises if you are struggling with the visioning exercise.

Visioning Bridge Exercise #1:

Write the following headings on a piece of paper, leaving space between them:

- Vacations you'd like to take
- People you'd like to meet
- Foods you'd like to try
- Places you'd like to go
- Relationships you'd like to have
- Hobbies you'd like to try

- Traits you'd like to develop (patience, love, and so on)
- Things you'd like to own
- Experiences you'd like to have
- Things you'd like to do with your children/spouse/friends/parents/relatives
- Add a few of your own categories

Take fifteen minutes each week to sit down and thoughtfully add items under the headings. After you have added a few items, select one to work with. Close your eyes, and do your best to imagine yourself in this experience. Try to be as detailed as possible, picturing what you might be seeing, doing, saying, smelling, or feeling in the moment.

Visioning Bridge Exercise #2:

Think of someone who has a life you really admire and would love to live. He or she could be famous or not. Reflect on this person's life, and take fifteen minutes to make a list of all the good things you imagine this person must be living. It is not important whether the items on your list are true or not. For example, if you pick Oprah Winfrey, you may list things like, "Her work is fascinating, she meets all kinds of interesting people, she lives in the most beautiful homes, she has seemingly thousands of friends, she has people who cook and clean for her and take care of her every need, she takes amazing vacations."

The following week, go back to the list you made and spend fifteen minutes on the next activity. Pick two things you wrote on the list, and imagine what it would be like if you actually had those things happen in your life. For example, you might select the fact that she meets with all kinds of interesting people, and take a few minutes to close your eyes and imagine what that might be like. Imagine yourself going up to a famous person you admire and having a conversation, or interviewing someone you've always wanted to meet. Really try to put yourself in the situation and feel the excitement of what that would be like. Make it as real as possible.

Continue doing this exercise each week for fifteen minute intervals until it gets easier. This will begin exercising your imagination and get you thinking outside the box for possible futures. After doing one or both of these bridging exercises for a few weeks, try the original visioning exercise again. Keep working at it until you can do the original exercise and really feel the emotion around your vision.

Appreciative Living 3-Step Model

The following Appreciative Living 3-Step Model[64] was adapted from the one I created in my book *Appreciative Living* as a simple way to apply the principles of Appreciative Inquiry to any situation.

The first step in the model is Appreciating What Is; the essence of this step is finding what is right or good about whatever is showing up. The outcome of this step is *feeling good* about what is happening. One of the most powerful exercises in this step is the gratitude list, which helps focus attention on positive aspects.

The second step is Imagining the Ideal, which is about creating mental pictures of our ideal experiences with whatever has come our way. The outcome of this step is getting clear about what we really want. Visualization is a key exercise in this step.

The final step is Acting in Alignment, which implores us to act and think in ways that align with what we want most. The goal of this step is to take action that moves us closer to what we desire, and the action most often taken is a deliberate change in thinking. The daily question is one of the most powerful exercises in this step, helping us define and create the changes that will make the biggest difference.

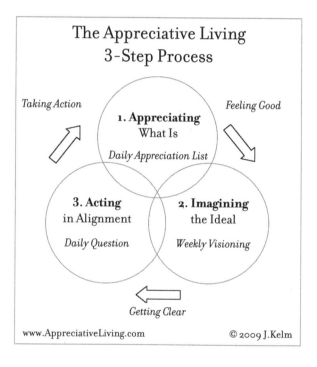

To learn more about the 3-Step Model and the principles of Appreciative Living, and to get a free copy of "Appreciative Living: Getting Started," visit www.AppreciativeLiving.com.

Questions for Reframing Difficult Situations

Use these questions to help appreciatively reframe a situation (pages 44–49):

- What strengths does this situation/person have, and what is good about it/him or her?
- What do I like about the situation/person?
- What do I stand to learn or gain from this?
- In what ways will my life be better after having worked through this?
- Who do I know who deals well with these types of situations, and what can I learn from him or her?
- When was a time in the past when I dealt successfully with a similar situation, and what can I apply from that?

- What are my greatest strengths, and how can I use them to help me in this situation?
- What am I excited or curious about in all this?
- What are two good things that could possibly come out of this?
- What are three reasons why I'm glad this situation has come up?
- How does this situation make me appreciate other people in my life even more?
- How will the learning from this situation spill over into other areas of my life?
- What am I grateful for in all of this?

Oxford Happiness Questionnaire[65]

By Peter Hills and Michael Argyle. Reprinted with permission from Elsevier Ltd. The Oxford Happiness Project, School of Psychology, Oxford Brookes University, UK

You can also take the questionnaire online for free at www.AppreciativeLiving.com.

Instructions: Below are a number of statements about happiness. Would you please indicate how much you agree or disagree with each by entering a number alongside it according to the following code:

1 = strongly disagree   2 = moderately disagree
3 = slightly disagree   4 = slightly agree
5 = moderately agree   6 = strongly agree

You will need to read the statements carefully because some are phrased positively and others negatively. Don't take too long over individual questions; there are no "right" or "wrong" answers and no trick questions. The first answer that comes into your head is probably the right one for you. If you find some of the questions difficult, please give the answer that is true for you in general or for most of the time.

_____   1.   I don't feel particularly pleased with the way I am (-)

_____   2.   I am intensely interested in other people

_____   3.   I feel that life is very rewarding

_____   4.   I have very warm feelings toward almost everyone

_____   5.   I rarely wake up feeling rested (-)

_____   6.   I am not particularly optimistic about the future (-)

_____   7.   I find most things amusing

_____   8.   I am always committed and involved

_____   9.   Life is good

_____   10. I do not think that the world is a good place (-)

_____   11. I laugh a lot

_____   12. I am well satisfied about everything in my life

_____   13. I don't think I look attractive (-)

_____   14. There is a gap between what I would like to do and what I have done (-)

_____   15. I am very happy

_____   16. I find beauty in some things

_____   17. I always have a cheerful effect on others

_____   18. I can fit in everything I want to

_____   19. I feel that I am not especially in control of my life (-)

_____   20. I feel able to take anything on

_____   21. I feel fully mentally alert

_____   22. I often experience joy and elation

_____   23. I do not find it easy to make decisions (-)

_____   24. I do not have a particular sense of meaning and purpose in my life (-)

_____ 25. I feel I have a great deal of energy

_____ 26. I usually have a good influence on events

_____ 27. I do not have fun with other people (-)

_____ 28. I don't feel particularly healthy (-)

_____ 29. I do not have particularly happy memories of the
          past (-)

Scoring. All 12 statements with a (-) after them need to be
reverse scored. For example,

    If you originally wrote "1" cross it out and write in a "6"

    If you originally wrote "2" cross it out and write in a "5"

    If you originally wrote "3" cross it out and write in a "4"

    If you originally wrote "4" cross it out and write in a "3"

    If you originally wrote "5" cross it out and write in a "2"

    If you originally wrote "6" cross it out and write in a "1"

After you have reverse scored these 12 statements, add the values for all 29 statements up. Then divide the total by 29. This is your overall measure of happiness. Your score will be somewhere between 1 and 6, and the higher the number, the happier you are.

Seven Discipline Dos Summary

*Use these tips to help you stay disciplined
in doing the exercises.*

1. Create Positive Rituals

Specify exactly when, where, and how you will do the exercises
ahead of time.

2. Track Your Results

- Do the weekly assessment in place of the daily exercises
  once a week
- Do the monthly assessment in place of the visioning
  exercise once a month
- Consider creating a checklist and marking it off each
  day after doing the exercises
- Periodically review what you've written

3. Reward Your Success

Make a list of activities you enjoy. Select one each week, and use it to reward yourself at the end if you do the exercises diligently. You can also reward yourself every couple of days if you feel your interest in the exercises is slipping, or frankly if you just want to up the joy in your life.

4. Create Novelty

If you begin to tire of the exercises, try the variations listed in Appendix B. You can also try your own modifications, but be sure to maintain the integrity of all three exercises.

5. Get Inspired

Reconnect regularly to your vision to keep motivated. If it no longer seems to inspire you, then you need to create a new one.

6. Partner with Someone or Join a Group

Find a friend and do the exercises together, or join an Appreciative Living Learning Circle at www.AppreciativeLiving.com.

7. Do It Anyway

Remember: *You always have time for the things you put first.*

Five Stages of Deliberate Change

Stage 1: Awareness—Recognizing that something in your life is not bringing joy

Stage 2: Commitment—Deciding and committing to create *more* of what you want

Stage 3: Action—Using the exercises to create what you want *more of*

- Appreciation List: Look for what you want more of, and write it down and appreciate it when you see it.

- Daily Question: Ask what one thing you can do, no matter how small, to create what you want more of.
- Visioning Exercise: Create an ideal vision of what you want more of.

Stage 4: Acclimation/Purging—Adjusting to the new and letting go of the old

Stage 5: Realization—Living into the new way of being

Joy Study Results Summary

Effects of Three Joy-Focused Exercises
on Overall Happiness

Jacqueline Kelm, MBA, CLL
April 2007

Abstract

A study was conducted with thirty participants to measure the impact of performing three psychological exercises on individual happiness. The results showed a significant increase in happiness levels after four weeks of doing the exercises, and the increase was sustained five months later.

Two trends concerning exercise persistence were observed. First, people who were most unhappy at the beginning of the study seemed to have the largest improvement in happiness, with the average person moving from the "unhappy" bottom half of the scale into the "happy" top half after four weeks. The second trend showed that those who continued to do the exercises had continued gains in their level of happiness, while those who stopped the exercises had a slight decline in overall happiness by the end of the third month. Nevertheless, both the participants who continued the exercises and those who stopped after the first month were still significantly happier six months after the study began than when they started. Interestingly, it was the people who were happiest at the start of the study who tended to continue the exercises on their own even though they experienced the smallest relative change. This continuation trend could not be significantly validated due to the unequal and relatively small sample sizes of the participant groups. Follow-up studies that examine these trends are fruitful areas for further investigation.

Participants performed two daily exercises that consisted of writing a gratitude list and answering a simple question on how they could increase joy for that day. The third exercise was a weekly fifteen-minute visioning session, where participants imagined and wrote about their ideal, joy-filled life.

Written assessments were completed by all thirty participants at study end, and phone interviews were conducted with twenty-two of them. The depth and breadth of these qualitative results was extensive, and the major themes identified follow:

1. People began to notice and experience more good in their lives.
2. Many got clearer about what they really wanted.
3. People learned what brought them joy and how to increase joy.
4. The exercises raised personal awareness and created a variety of meaningful insights.

5. Many came to understand they were responsible for creating their own happiness.

6. The exercises were used as tools in dealing with difficulties.

7. The morning exercises were instrumental in setting up a good day.

8. Rituals were helpful in keeping up with the exercises.

For more information visit: www.AppreciativeLiving.com, or send an e-mail to Admin@AppreciativeLiving.com.

The Participants

There were forty-four people initially in the study, but only thirty of them successfully completed all the requirements. The majority of participants were solicited via e-mail from a list of people who had purchased the book *Appreciative Living* or attended a workshop. The remaining individuals were friends and relatives of these same people. To this extent, participants were biased in that they were people who desired an increase in joy in their lives. Since this is the target population for this work, the bias should not adversely affect results.

Participants were primarily female, Caucasian, in the 30 to 50 age group, with an undergraduate or graduate college degree. They were also a relatively happy group, with 73 percent of participants rating themselves between slightly and extremely happy at the study start. The detailed breakout of demographics follows:

30 Participants total: 7 men and 23 women

Ages:

>   11 in the 30 to 39 group
>   11 in the 40 to 49 group
>   7 in the 50 to 59 group
>   1 in the over 60 group

Locations: (10 different states plus Canada)

>   13 from North Carolina
>   5 from Washington State
>   4 from Ohio
>   1 from Canada
>   1 each from Utah, Rhode Island, Pennsylvania, Michigan,
>   Alaska, California, and New Hampshire

Partnership Status:

>   21 married
>   7 Single
>   1 polygamous
>   1 in partnership

Religious Affiliation:

>   6 No affiliation
>   6 Unity/New Thought
>   4 Pagan

3 Catholic

3 Christian

3 Unitarian Universalist

1 Agnostic

1 Religious science

1 Protestant-Presbyterian

1 Church of Jesus Christ of Latter-day Saints

1 Independent

Race

2 Hispanic

3 Black/Biracial

25 White

Highest Education

2 High school

10 Undergraduate

12 Graduate

6 Post graduate

The Study Process

Participants were asked to begin on July 16, 2006 by completing the Fordyce Emotions Questionnaire,[66] which is a simple scale for measuring individual happiness. Two basic questions were asked. The first was to rate how happy you usually feel on a scale of 0 to 10, with 0 being extremely unhappy, 5 neutral, and 10 being extremely happy. Then you are asked to rate the percent of time on average you feel happy, neutral, and unhappy.

Participants were asked to complete exercises that would increase their joy (not happiness), but a comparable and commonly used evaluation for measuring joy could not be found. The Fordyce Emotions Questionnaire was used as a substitute, assuming a definition of joy to be an elevated level of happiness. The idea of measuring joy versus happiness was not an issue for most participants, who essentially felt an inherent, direct connection between the two. There were a few people who expressed frustration with the inability of the scale to truly assess the value of the change they experienced. The extent of learning and insights gained during the four weeks could not be fully captured by the simple scale. The qualitative section of this article attempts to identify some of this value. A more thorough scale, such as the Oxford Happiness Questionnaire, is recommended for future studies.[67]

The word *joy* was not defined in the study, which allowed participants to work with the concept in a way that was meaningful for them. In the written assessment they were asked to provide their working definition; most people described it as feeling good, and/or in a heightened state of happiness. Some defined it more as a state of being in either an ecstatic, blissful place or a peaceful, serene state. Several participants suggested that it would have been helpful to have a simple definition provided up front, and this would be recommended for further studies.

Upon completing the assessment, participants began a set of three exercises. On a daily basis they wrote three things they were grateful for, and then answered a question regarding one thing they could do that day to increase their joy. Once a week they did a fifteen-minute visioning exercise where they imagined and wrote about their ideal, joy-filled life.

Four weeks later, on August 13, 2006, they were asked to complete an ending assessment. This assessment included the same questions from the Fordyce Emotions Questionnaire to gather quantitative data, but also asked for written responses to questions about individual experiences to gather qualitative data. It included the following questions:

1. Please share at least one story of how these exercises positively impacted your life.
2. What insights did you have, or what did you learn while doing these exercises?
3. As you reflect on your four-week experience, how could these exercises have been even better?
4. How would you define joy in the way you thought of it each day as you were doing the question exercise?
5. Please list the dates on which you completed the four visioning exercises.
6. Did you miss any days of doing the daily gratitude and questioning exercises? If so, please list the dates you missed.
7. Was there any significant life event that occurred during these four weeks, such as a death, job loss, or special vacation at the end of study, etc., which might have affected your results?
8. Would you be willing to discuss your experience by phone interview?

Follow-up phone conversations were offered to all thirty participants, and twenty-two agreed to this to process their experience
more closely. The breadth and depth of the insights and learning people experienced were extensive, and are summarized in
the abstract. In addition to reporting an increase in perceived
happiness, they also described having learned important concepts regarding the nature of happiness and practical ways to
create more of it in their lives.

Participants completed a total of four follow-up assessments containing the basic numerical ratings from the Fordyce
Emotions Questionnaire. They were done one, two, three,
and six months after the study began, for a total of five data
points. Participants were not asked to continue the exercises
past four weeks, but the majority did of their own accord.

Quantitative Results

There was a significant increase in the overall percent of time
participants felt happy and a significant decrease in the percent
of time they experienced unhappiness. Figure 1 shows a 15 percent increase in the percent of time participants felt happy from
the study beginning to the end of six months, going from 48 percent to 67 percent (Wilks' Δ = .53, F = 5.77, p < .01). The percent
of time participants felt neutral dropped from 20 percent to 12
percent (Wilks' Δ= .69, F = 2.98, p < .05). The percent of time
being unhappy fell from 33 percent to 21 percent (Wilks' Δ = .60,
F = 4.40, p < .01). Follow-up pairwise comparisons indicated a
significant difference between the means for the start of the
study and each of the monthly time intervals. These findings

suggest that the changes in happiness percentages resulting from the exercises were sustained for the five months following the study.

Overall Average Percent Time Participants Felt Happy, Neutral, and Unhappy (n = 30)

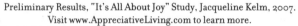

Preliminary Results, "It's All About Joy" Study, Jacqueline Kelm, 2007. Visit www.AppreciativeLiving.com to learn more.

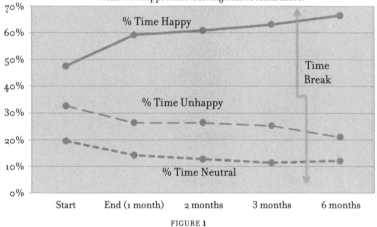

FIGURE 1

In their article "Positive Psychology Progress: Empirical Validation of Interventions,"[68] Seligman, Steen, and Peterson suggest that a placebo effect occurs in these types of interventions. They found that participants who did a "neutral" exercise during a similar study showed an increase in happiness while doing the exercises by virtue of being part of a study focused on creating happiness. However, the increase did not last, and placebo participants returned to their baseline happiness level within a week of the study end. Since participants in this joy study maintained significant elevated levels of happiness for five months following the study end, it is assumed this was not due to a placebo effect. There is also sufficient qualitative data to suggest that the exercises had a significant impact on individual happiness, since 67 percent of participants continued at least some of the exercises on their own for a period of time.

Figure 2 shows that the average happiness for the thirty participants increased significantly from 6.4 to 7.8 from study start to end (Wilks' Λ = .54, F = 5.46, p < .01). Pairwise comparisons show that the exercises did have a significant effect on happiness at the end of the first four weeks, and this effect was sustained for the next five months.

Interestingly, the largest average increase occurred with people who had initially assessed themselves in the lower half of the happiness scale. Those who rated themselves as neutral or unhappy at the study start went from an average happiness level of 3.4 to a remarkable 6.4 after the first month. People who rated themselves as happy at the study start (6 to 10 on the happiness scale) showed a much smaller increase in happiness, going from only 7.5 to 7.9. These results suggest that unhappy people may experience greater quantitative benefits from the exercises than happy people; however, because the sample sizes of these two groups were disproportionate, statistical tests were not meaningful. Further studies need to be done to confirm these findings statistically.

In Figure 3, the happiness levels are shown for those who completed none, some, or all of the exercises after the first four weeks. This data was only analyzed for the first three months following the study since the number of people doing exercises on their own began to fall off. Those who did some of the exercises

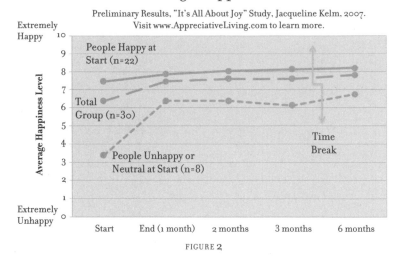

FIGURE 2

were doing a range of combinations and frequencies. ANOVA was conducted to evaluate the relationship between continuing to do the exercises and the overall level of happiness, and indicated that there is a relationship between the second and third months. That is the difference in overall happiness levels between those who continue doing the exercises and those who do not increases as time proceeds. In fact, 23 percent of the difference in overall happiness levels for the second month and 29 percent of the difference for the third month is related to whether a person continued to do an exercise or not. An important caveat to these findings is that the sample sizes were small and unequal, so further studies will need to be done to determine statistical significance.

Another interesting observation from this graph is that the people who tended to continue the exercises were those

Average Happiness of Those Who Continued to Do All, Some, or No Exercises Past the First Month

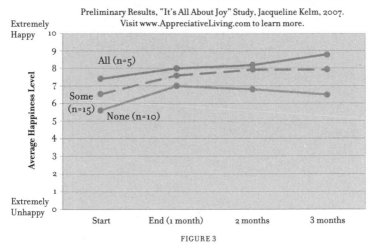

Preliminary Results, "It's All About Joy" Study, Jacqueline Kelm, 2007.
Visit www.AppreciativeLiving.com to learn more.

FIGURE 3

who started out happier, and those who continued all the exercises tended to be the happiest at the start. Given the relatively larger increase in happiness experienced by those who were most unhappy at the start, this is an intriguing development. It appears that those who are most happy in general are more likely to engage in these types of exercises. It is plausible to believe that the experience of going from 3.4 to 6.4 on the happiness scale would be a stronger motivator to continue the exercises than going from 7.4 to 8, yet this was not the case.

Conclusion

Performing the joy exercises for four weeks made people significantly happier, and this elevated state remained for five months.

Two interesting trends were observed in terms of who continued
the exercises on their own and who benefited most; these could
be explored in follow-up studies. A number of significant and
meaningful insights were reported by many participants, and
some described them as life-altering. Please contact Admin@
AppreciativeLiving.com for more information.

{ Notes }

1. Pearsall, Paul (2003). *The Beethoven Factor: The New Positive Psychology of Hardiness Happiness, Healing, and Hope.* Charlottesville, VA: Hampton Roads Publishing, p. xi.

2. Cooperrider, David, and Diana Whitney (1999). *Appreciative Inquiry: A Positive Revolution in Change.* San Francisco, CA: Berrett-Koehler.

3. MSNBC (1/24/05). Retrieved on (3/24/08) www.msnbc.msn.com/jd/6847012.

4. Wikipedia. Retrieved on (3/15/08) http://en.wikipedia.org/wiki/Blue_Monday.

5. Cooperrider and Whitney, *Appreciative Inquiry: A Positive Revolution in Change*, pp. 14–17.

6. Kelm, Jacqueline (2005). *Appreciative Living: The Principles of Appreciative Inquiry in Personal Life.* Wake Forest, NC: Venet Publishers, pp. 113–45.

7. Nelson, Noelle, and Jeannine Calaba (2003). *The Power of Appreciation: The Key to a Vibrant Life.* Hillsboro, OR: Beyond Words Publishing, p. 24.

8. I have found meditation to be incredibly helpful in learning to detach from my stories. There are many different practices and philosophies for meditating, and just about any one can work to slow down your thinking and detach from your experience. A good book for getting started is *Eight Minute Meditation* by Victor Davish.

9. Gilbert, Daniel (2006). *Stumbling on Happiness.* New York: Alfred A. Knopf, p. 168.

10. Gilbert, Rosalene (2002). *Optimal Thinking: How to be Your Best Self.* New York: Wiley & Sons, Inc., p. 98.

11. Doidge, Norman (2007). *The Brain That Changes Itself: Stories of Personal Triumph from the Frontiers of Brain Science.* New York: The Penguin Group, pp. 203–04.

12. Begley, Sharon (2007). *Train York Mind, Change Your Brain: How a New Science Reveals Our Extraordinary Potential to Transform Ourselves.* New York: Ballantine Books, p. 9.

13. Cooper, Robert (2006). *Get Out of Your Own Way: The 5 Keys to Surpassing Everyone's Expectations.* New York: Crown Business, p. 34.

14. Cooperrider, David (1990). "Positive Image, Positive Action: The Affirmative Basis of Organizing," in *Appreciative Management and Leadership.* San Francisco, CA: Jossey-Bass, p. 119. This article is also available online at http://appreciativeinquiry. case.edu/.

15. Lyubomirsky, Sonja (2008). *The How of Happiness: A Scientific Approach to Getting the Life You Want.* New York: Penguin Press, p. 111.

16. Willamson, Marianne (1991). *A Return to Love: Reflections on the Principles of A Course in Miracles.* New York: Harper Collins. pp. 190–91.

17. Seligman, Martin E. P. (2002). *Authentic Happiness: Using the New Positive Psychology to Realize Your Potential for Lasting Fulfillment.* New York: Simon & Schuster, pp. 40–41.

18. Fredrickson, Barbara, L. (2001). "The Role of Positive Emotions in Positive Psychology." *American Psychologist,* 56(3), p. 219.

19. Katie, Byron (2002). *Loving What Is: Four Questions That Can Change Your Life.* New York: Three Rivers Press, p. 135.

20. Whitney, Diana, and Amanda Trosten-Bloom (2003). *The Power of Appreciative Inquiry: A Practical Guide to Positive Change.* San Francisco, CA: Berrett-Koehler, p. 67.

21. The largest study of average happiness over time was done with two thousand healthy veterans of World War II and the Korean War. It showed that life satisfaction actually increased from age forty until around age sixty-five, and then began to decline slightly, with a significant decline around age seventy-five. These graphs do not account for these changes since the purpose is to show the relative comparison, so the potential age effects were not factored in. Happiness over time data from Sonja Lyubomirsky's *The How of Happiness,* pp. 63–64.

22. This is a preliminary hypothesis based on my personal experience. There are very few people who have actually embarked on an intentional path to shift their thinking toward happiness, so I could not find readily available data on what the path looks like. It is relatively uncharted ter-

ritory, but hopefully more data will become available.

23. Seligman, *Authentic Happiness*, p. 48.

24. Walker, Lucy (September 10, 2006). "Westerners Can't Just Succeed Anymore." *Toronto Star*, p. D1.

25. Greene, Bob (2006). *The Best Life Diet*. New York: Simon & Schuster, p. 22.

26. Ibid., p. 26.

27. Lyubomirsky, *The How of Happiness*, pp. 52–55.

28. Ibid., pp. 38–41.

29. Doidge,. *The Brain That Changes Itself*, pp. xvii–xx.

30. Rinpoche, Yongey Mingyur (2007). *The Joy of Living: Unlocking the Secret and Science of Happiness*. New York: Harmony Books, pp. 3–4.

31. Doidge, *The Brain That Changes Itself*, pp. 199–200.

32. Begley, *Train Your Mind, Change Your Brain*, p. 231.

33. Fredrickson, "The Role of Positive Emotions in Positive Psychology," p. 219.

34. Fredrickson, Barbara, L. (2003). "Positive Emotions and Upward Spirals in Organizational Settings." From Cameron, K., J. Dutton, and R. Quinn, *Positive Organizational Scholarship*. San Francisco, CA: Berrett-Koehler, p. 169.

35. Seligman, *Authentic Happiness*, pp. 102–11.

36. Ibid., pp. 111–21.

37. Csíkszentmihályi, Mihály (1996). *Flow: The Psychology of Optimal Experi-ence*. New York: HarperCollins, pp. 45–93.

38. Ben-Shahar, Tal (2007). *Happier: Learn the Secrets to Daily Joy and Lasting Fulfillment*. New York: McGraw-Hill, p. 33.

39. Ibid., p. 27.

40. Remen, Rachel N. (1996). *Kitchen Table Wisdom: Stories That Heal*. New York: Riverhead Books, pp. 171–72.

41. Doidge, *The Brain That Changes Itself*, p. 68.

42. Gilbert, *Stumbling on Happiness*, p. 210.

43. Ibid., p. 179.

44. Cooper, *Get Out of Your Own Way*, p. 35.

45. Ibid., p. 26.

46. Doidge, *The Brain That Changes Itself*, pp. 59–60.

47. Loehr, Jim, and Tony Schwartz (2003). *The Power of Full Engagement: Managing Energy, Not Time, Is the Key to High Performance and Personal Renewal*. New York: The Free Press, p. 14.

48. Ibid., pp. 14–15.

49. Ibid., pp. 175–76.

50. Ibid., p. 175.

51. Cooper, *Get Out of Your Own Way*, p. 270.

52. Doidge, *The Brain That Changes Itself*, p. 71.

53. Gilbert, *Stumbling on Happiness*, p. 130.

54. Cooper, *Get Out of Your Own Way*, p. 278.

55. Ibid., pp. 278–79.

56. Article from the WeightWatchers website extracted (2/18/08): "New

Study Shows Attendance at Weight-Watchers Meetings Strongly Linked to Weight Loss and Health Improvements," www.weightwatchers.com/util/art/index_art.aspx?art_id=33481&tabnum=1&sc=808&subnav=In+the+Spotlight.

57. Doidge, *The Brain That Changes Itself*, pp. 199–200.

58. Yeager, Selene (November 2007). "Exercise: The Least You Can Do." *O Magazine*, pp. 201–02.

59. Church, T. S., C. P. Earnest, J. S. Skinner, and S. N. Blair (2007). "Effects of Different Doses of Physical Activity on Cardiorespiratory Fitness Among Sedentary, Overweight or Obese Postmenopausal Women with Elevated Blood Pressure." *Journal of the American Medical Association*, 297: pp. 2081–91.

60. Cooperrider, David, and Suresh Srivastva (1987). *Appreciative Inquiry in Organizational Life*. Research in Organization Change and Development. Vol. 1. Edited by W. Pasmore and R. Woodman. JAI Press. This article can also be found at the AI Commons website, http://appreciativeinquiry.case.edu.

61. Watkins, Jane and Bernard Mohr (2001). *Appreciative Inquiry: Change at the Speed of Imagination*. San Francisco, CA: Jossey-Bass/Pfeiffer, p. 15.

62. Whitney, Diana, and Amanda Trosten-Bloom (2003). *The Power of Appreciative Inquiry: A Practical Guide for Positive Change*. San Francisco, CA: Berrett-Koehler, p. 1.

63. Hammond, Susan A. (1996). *The Thin Book of Appreciative Inquiry*. Plano, TX: Kodiak Consulting. pp. 20–21.

64. Adapted from Kelm, Jacqueline (2005). *Appreciative Living: The Principles of Appreciative Inquiry in Personal Life*. Wake Forest, NC: Venet Publishers, pp. 145–55.

65. Hills, Peter, and Michael Argyle (2002). "The Oxford Happiness Questionnaire." *Personality and Individual Differences*, 33, pp. 1073–82. Reprinted with permission of Elsevier Ltd.

66. Fordyce, Michael (1988). "A Review of Research on the Happiness Measures: A Sixty-Second Index of Happiness and Mental Health." *Social Indicators Research*, 20, pp. 355–81.

67. Hills and Argyle, "The Oxford Happiness Questionnaire," pp. 1073–82.

68. Seligman, M.E., T. A. Steen, and C. Peterson (2005). "Positive Psychology Progress: Empirical Validation of Interventions." *American Psychologist*, 60(5), pp. 410–21.

{ Index }

ABOUT THE AUTHOR

Jackie Kelm is a speaker, coach, and author of the book *Appreciative Living: The Principles of Appreciative Inquiry in Personal Life*. She holds a B.S. in mechanical engineering and an MBA from Case Western Reserve University. While passionate about sharing her work, she thoroughly enjoys life with her husband and two children. She can be reached at www.AppreciativeLiving.com.